Tidewater Virginia

With Children

Where to Go and What to Do
in Williamsburg, Jamestown,
Yorktown, Newport News, and Hampton

Barbara M. Wohlford
and Mary L. Eley

Camino Books, Inc.
PHILADELPHIA

Manufactured in the United States of America

1 2 3 4 5   99   98 97 96

Library of Congress Cataloging-in-Publication Data

Wohlford, Barbara M.
   Tidewater Virginia with children: where to go and what to
do in Williamsburg, Jamestown, Yorktown and Newport News
by Barbara M. Wohlford and Mary L. Eley.
    p. cm.
   Includes index.
   ISBN 0-940159-38-4
   1. Tidewater (VA. : Region)—Guidebooks. 2. Family
recreation—Virginia—Tidewater (Region)—Guidebooks
   I. Eley, Mary L.
   II. Title.
   F232.T54W64 1996
   917.55'10443—dc20   96-6883

Cover and interior design: Robert LeBrun

This book is available at a special discount on bulk purchases
for promotional, business and educational use.

For information, write to:

Publisher
Camino Books, Inc.
P.O. Box 59026
Philadelphia, PA 19102

We would like to express our appreciation to computer gurus Scott and Melissa Benson, George Greenia, and Tom Wood for their support of the "technology challenged" writers.

We also would like to express a special thank you to our husbands Jack Wohlford and Claude Eley for their support, encouragement, and good humor throughout this project.

Dedicated to Our Grandchildren

Contents

Getting Started

Whatever your definition of family fun, it seems likely you'll find it here in Tidewater Virginia.

If you like history, there's the understated mystery of a morning stroll along the quaint streets of Colonial Williamsburg, where you can move among the three-cornered hats and mob caps to sample American culture preserved just as it was in the eighteenth century.

If Williamsburg's too modern for your family's taste, you might try browsing through the early seventeenth century, taking time to explore life in the Indian huts at Jamestown, or snooping below deck of the *Susan Constant*, one of the three ships moored at the nearby English settlement.

Perhaps your family is more interested in nature. You might just be lucky enough to encounter the unbending gaze of a hawk while you amble about the grounds of the Virginia Living Museum. While there, you could revel in the many species of birds in residence, or have a chat with the red fox, or dip your hand into the "touch tank" to examine a sea critter.

Looking for summer relief? Try the wet and refreshing jolt of a twisting, screaming slide at Water Country USA.

For something more serious, spend an hour taking in a film on the earth's environment at the Virginia Air and Space Center's IMAX Theatre.

And for the perfect nightcap to a busy day, try a moonlit run on the Big Bad Wolf at Busch Gardens. Sit back for a wild ride that rises along the giant treetops, then plunges to the sparkling river below, only to rush back up again, twisting and turning through the trees. Grandma never envisioned a scare this big.

Still not had enough? Well, you've only scratched the surface of where Old Virginia and New Virginia meet to present the best of nature, history, technology, and fantasy. It's all conveniently situated along one 60-mile stretch of Interstate 64, running from the pine forests and gentle countryside of Williamsburg down to the lapping waters of Chesapeake Bay.

The pages of this book are filled with ideas for places to take children that can be enjoyed by the entire family. Whenever possible, we have tried to indicate attractions and restaurants that are located in the same vicinity to facilitate the planning of a full day's outing. However, please remember that the cornerstone for successful family outings is to plan ahead.

In this section is a list of newspapers and magazines that publish current information regarding activities on the Peninsula. Also included are some useful telephone numbers, transportation information, a listing of information centers and services, as well as suggestions for a three-day tour of the area.

Throughout the book we have tried to be as accurate as possible with the information we supply. However, it is always a good idea to call your destinations in advance.

Have a wonderful time!

Newspapers and Magazines

Colonial Guide

A free magazine readily available at most stores and restaurants. Published monthly, the Guide lists local attractions and restaurants, and also contains discount coupons.

Colonial Williamsburg Calendar

This free calendar lists, one month in advance, the events and activities taking place in the Historic Area.

Colonial Williamsburg Visitor's Companion

Published weekly, this publication describes the events and attractions in Colonial Williamsburg for the current week and is available at the Colonial Williamsburg Visitor Center and at various other sites in the Historic Area.

Daily Press

Published daily, it is the area's leading newspaper.

Port Folio

Published monthly, this free newspaper is a guide to restaurants, activities, and entertainment in Williamsburg, Newport News, Hampton, Virginia Beach, and Norfolk.

Inroads

Included as a special section in the Daily Press every Friday, *Inroads* contains an area calendar of music, theatre, and dance, as well as a guide to restaurants in Hampton, Newport News, Williamsburg, Norfolk, Virginia Beach, and Portsmouth.

Virginia Gazette

Published Wednesday and Saturday, this newspaper prints a current listing of the events and activities in the Williamsburg area.

Williamsburg Magazine

This free magazine is published the first of every month and is available in most stores and restaurants.

Williamsburg—Virginia's Great Entertainer

Published three times per year, this colorful and informative magazine makes a nice souvenir. It offers a description of the activities, entertainment, and restaurants in Williamsburg. Free.

Useful Information

Note that the area code for the Peninsula is 804 but will be changed to 757 on July 1, 1996.

Time of day
229-1140.

Local Weather
877-1221.

Youth Services

Big Brothers/Big Sisters 253-0676.

Boy Scouts Colonial Virginia Council 877-5085.

Child Development Resources 565-0303.

Girl Scouts Council of Colonial Coast 1-800-77SCOUT.

Physicians Referral Service 1-800-468-0199.

Dental Referral Service (757) 874-0562.

Transportation

An automobile is almost a necessity for touring the Peninsula, but some public transportation is available.

Colonial Williamsburg

Colonial Williamsburg operates a bus for Colonial Williamsburg ticket holders. The bus route brings riders from the Visitor Center to the Historic Area with frequent stops in the Historic Area.

Greyhound Bus

Williamsburg Station 468 N. Boundary St. 229-1460.

Hampton Station 22 S. Armistead Ave. 722-9861.

Newport News Station 9702 Jefferson Ave. 599-3900.

James City County Transit Co.

Call 220-1621 for fares and schedules. The company also operates a paratransit service for disabled persons who cannot use the regular bus service.

Jamestown Ferry

The ferry connects Jamestown to Scotland Wharf, Surry. It operates daily from 5:00 a.m. to midnight. Call 229-4193 for fare and schedule information.

Newport News/Williamsburg International Airport
Bland Blvd. off Jefferson Ave., Newport News 877-0221.

Pentran
Operates on the Peninsula. Call 723-3344 for fare and schedule information.

Information Centers and Services

Colonial Williamsburg Visitor Center
Route 132Y and the Colonial Parkway (757) 220-7643.

Hampton Visitor Center
710 Settler's Landing Road (757) 727-1102 or 1-800-800-2202.

Newport News Public Information and Community Relations
(757) 247-2616.

Peninsula Tourism and Conference Center
Christopher Newport University, Newport News (757) 886-7777.

Virginia Peninsula Tourist Information Center
Newport News Park (757) 886-7777.

Williamsburg Area Convention and Visitor Center
(757) 253-0192.

Williamsburg Chamber of Commerce
201 Penniman Road (757) 229-6511.

Library for the Blind
Central Library, 4207 Victoria Blvd., Hampton (757) 727-1900.

Library for the Blind and Physically Handicapped
112 Main Street, Newport News (757) 886-7999.

Doing the Peninsula in Three Days

A whirlwind three-day tour of the Peninsula can be lots of fun if three important points are remembered: (1) set an agreeable pace, (2) wear comfortable shoes and bring along a stroller for the youngest visitors, and (3) vary the activities to keep up interest and enthusiasm. The suggestions below are proposed with warm-weather touring in mind and are offered just as a guide to planning your own itinerary.

Day One

Depending on time, the age of the children, and your interests, you may want to purchase a one-day ticket to Colonial Williamsburg. This ticket permits entry to many of the buildings and trade shops. Or just spend the morning walking about the eighteenth century town, visit a garden or two, buy tickets for a horse-drawn carriage ride, and shop in Merchants Square. Whichever choice you make, be sure to make lunch reservations at one of the Colonial Williamsburg taverns to sample how colonial Virginians took their meals. A 15-minute drive down the Colonial Parkway to Jamestown Settlement is a delightful way to spend the afternoon. See the next section for details regarding both of these outstanding indoor/outdoor museums. After dinner, top off the evening with a foot-stomping visit to the Old Dominion Opry (see page 59).

Day Two

Dress comfortably and enjoy a fun-filled day at Busch Gardens. This is one of the outstanding theme parks in the country and will be enjoyed by the whole family. There are many places for lunch and dinner in the park. If time and energy permit, consider buying a combination ticket to Busch Gardens and Water Country USA in order to sample the noteworthy features of both parks. See page 50 for details.

Day Three

The Virginia Air and Space Center, located on the waterfront in Hampton, is a fascinating and unique place to begin the day. While touring the captivating exhibits, be sure to allow enough time to see the film in the impressive IMAX theatre (see page 33).

Grab a hot dog for lunch and then ride the antique carousel located adjacent to the Air and Space Center. Next on the program might be a relaxing harbor cruise on the *Miss Hampton II* docked on the waterfront close to Carousel Park (page 49).

Another option for day three could be a visit to the Virginia Living Museum in Newport News. One of the Peninsula's unusual and exciting museums, it offers fascinating indoor and outdoor exhibits (see page 36). For something different, pack a picnic lunch to bring along and enjoy at nearby Deer Run Park, or stop for a meal at close-by Ryan's Steak House. The Mariner's Museum, situated just down Route 17, is a treat for the whole family. End the day by cheering on one of the Peninsula's professional ball teams or teeing off for some miniature golf.

Museums

Your children may equate the word museum with dusty boredom, but the museums in this section have a depth—not just of content and scholarship—but of space itself, allowing you to get lost in a maze of time, as if entering a new dimension.

The multifaceted museum at Jamestown Settlement is one possibility that lets you do just that. While it tells the story of Virginia's early English settlement (begun in 1607), the museum also wonderfully captures the three cultures—Native American, European, and African—that meshed in and around Jamestown during the seventeenth century. The fascinating background material on the Powhatan Indians and their ancestors runs back 10,000 years. This museum is no lightweight experience; it will leave you and your children with a broader understanding of modern culture.

Jamestown is also plenty of fun as are the numerous other museum suggestions in this section. Colonial Williamsburg; the Virginia Living Museum, home to hundreds of species of birds, fish, and animals; and the Virginia Air and Space Center, filled with real live space vehicles and airplanes, are other standouts.

To help you decide where to begin, the top museums are listed alphabetically and by area. Try combining this section with a nature or park choice (See "Parks, Nature, and Beaches") for a full day's outing. However, do note that many of the indoor/outdoor museums and the larger museums are full-day outings in themselves.

The Historic Triangle:
Williamsburg, Jamestown, and Yorktown

America's Railroads on Parade

Village Shops at Kingsmill on Route 60. (757-220-TRAK)

Follow I-64 to exit 242A. Follow Route 60 East to shopping mall on left.

- Open daily 9:00 a.m. to 8:00 p.m.
- Adults $5.00, children (3-18) $2.50. Variety of discounts available.
- "Hands-on" exhibits.

Forty-six model trains of various sizes operate simultaneously on multi-level remote-controlled layouts. The layouts and dioramas designed by Broadway set designers are fascinating in their own right. The story of the construction of the elaborate trestle bridge is fascinating. A narrated tour lasts about 30 minutes. The two "hands-on" exhibits are a particular delight for the youngest railroad buffs. A small retail area sells train memorabilia but does not sell model trains.

Colonial Williamsburg

Williamsburg (757-229-1000).

Follow the green and white Colonial Williamsburg directional signs located on all access roads in the area (exits 238A or 242A off I-64) to the Visitor Center on Information Drive (Route 132Y). The Visitor Center is open daily 8:30 a.m. to 7:00 p.m. From January to mid-March it is open 9:00 a.m. to 5:00 p.m.

- Open daily year round; summer: 9:30 a.m. to 5:30 p.m., winter: 9:30 a.m. to 4:30 p.m. Exceptions are noted in the Visitor's Companion.

- Ticket options: The Patriot Pass permits unlimited entry into all Historic Area homes, trade shops, buildings, Carter's Grove Plantation, and is good for one full year (see Carter's Grove Plantation, page 42). Adults $33.00, children (6-12) $19.00, children under 6 are free. The Basic Admission Ticket is a one-day ticket and includes a choice of exhibits in the Historic Area. (Note: several of the major exhibition buildings and museums are not included.) Adults $25.00, children (6-12) $15.00, children under 6 are free. The Basics Plus Ticket is a two-day ticket and does not include Bassett Hall. Adults $29.00, children (6-12) $17.00. All rates are subject to change.

- Visitor's Companion. A weekly scheduled listing of events, dates, and times. Available with Historic Area map at time of ticket purchase and to non-ticket holders on request.
- Free parking at Visitor Center and bus to Historic Area with ticket purchase.
- Handicapped accessible. Building accessibility information available at the Visitor Center. Call 220-7645 for further information. A limited number of wheelchairs are available at the Visitor Center. Strollers are available at the Williamsburg Lodge.
- School tours. Call 229-1000 for information.
- Children and family tours and programs available in June, July, and August. Call 220-7645 for program information throughout the year and always check the Visitor's Companion for updated information.

Colonial Williamsburg has set the worldwide standard for historical restoration. It is a living, indoor/outdoor museum that immerses the visitor in the eighteenth century. It is complete with homes of the gentry class, those of the "middlin" sort, and historic trade shops. Extremely knowledgeable, costumed interpreters guide visitors through the homes and buildings, relate information about the history, furnishings, and occupants, and can answer most questions. Be sure to visit the wide variety of trade shops and watch skilled, costumed trades men and women accomplish their tasks in the eighteenth-century manner. It is fascinating to watch them work and visitors (including children) are often invited to participate.

The following tours and programs as well as many others are all described in the Visitor's Companion. Visitors receive this schedule as well as a map of the Historic Area when purchasing tickets. The Visitor's Companion is also available to non-ticket holders on request. Be advised that most of the programs described below take place during the summer months of June, July, and August. To avoid possible disappointment, always check the Visitor's Companion for programming information.

Start your tour by seeing the 35-minute orientation film, *Williamsburg—The Story of a Patriot*, shown at the Visitor Center. After purchasing your admission ticket, board the bus to the Historic Area and stop first at the Benjamin Powell House. While here, help the Powells with their daily life activities such as watering the garden, shaking out bed linens, setting the table for dinner, or playing board games.

Join one of the Family Participatory tours at the Capitol. Here is an opportunity to "become" an eighteenth-century citizen and take part in some of the activities of the Virginia House of Burgesses. Visit the Gaol where convicted felons were sent and help the costumed young interpreters there with family chores. At the Geddy House and Foundry, visitors may meet one of the 9- to 16-year-old apprentices who work in the shop. At the Wythe House, visitors may help with the animals in the stable or draw water from a well.

There are many other sites of interest to families. Ever help make a brick? You can try it at the Carpenter's Yard or observe how colonial woodworkers and carpenters plied their trades. Visitors to the Courthouse can "become" town citizens and take part in the reenactment of a county court session. (Check the Visitor's Companion for daily schedule.) The stocks and pillory located right outside the Courthouse are sure to be a favorite of the family photographer. Family activities are held in the garden at the Governor's Palace. Try out some of the eighteenth-century games and puzzles and listen to stories.

"Join" the Continental Army at the Military Encampment and experience the life of an eighteenth-century soldier. Those "enlisted" learn to march, handle "firearms," and fire the cannon. This tour lasts 45 minutes, so bear that in mind and consider your child's age and attention span.

If you want to rumble around in colonial fashion, take a ride in the stage wagon, Virginia wagon, or carriage. Tickets may be purchased at the Greenhow Lumber House.

The Capitol, Colonial Williamsburg. *Photograph by Marguerite Lamond.*

Lanthorn tours are another possibility for families. These tours consist of an evening walk through the streets and a visit to four candlelit trade shops. Tours leave the Greenhow Lumber House at 8:30 p.m. and cost $5.00 for Patriot Pass holders and $10.00 for non-Patriot Pass holders.

The Fife and Drum Parades are performed daily down Duke of Gloucester Street. This is a wonderful opportunity for children to see others of their age engaged in depicting the role children played in the colonial militia. Some evenings, there is a Military Review and the firing of the Evening Gun. Check the Visitor's Companion for daily schedule.

Of course, there are many illustrious as well as unfamiliar eighteenth-century citizens walking about town. Visitors may meet Thomas Jefferson, George Wythe, Grandma Geddy, tavernkeeper Jane Vobe, and others as they go about their daily lives. Do stop and chat with them. They are most interesting and enjoy meeting people.

There are several places to purchase children's books and gifts. The bookstore at the Visitor Center, the Craft House, and the stores and shops in the Historic Area carry many such items. The Little Patriot, a gift shop located across from the Visitor Center, features many items of interest to children.

Colonial Williamsburg also offers programs for children of guests staying at any of the Foundation's official hotels. The "clubs" are for children aged 5 to 12. Sign up for the mid-afternoon or evening sessions. A wide variety of activities are offered such as Historic Area tours, swimming, lawn bowling, and box lunches or dinners.

Fife and Drum Parade, Colonial Williamsburg. *Photograph by Barbara Wohlford.*

Please remember not to overdo it! Take a break after an hour or so. Pay a visit to the animals. Horses, sheep, ducks, geese, cows, oxen, and other animals are to be found throughout the town. Children will enjoy seeing them, but feeding or petting the animals is not permitted. Consider a visit to the College of William and Mary. Children might enjoy seeing where wealthy male children went to school in the eighteenth century. Take a lunch break at one of the Colonial Williamsburg taverns. (See listings in "Restaurants" for a delightful and unique colonial dining experience.)

Choose from a wide selection of building tours, trade demonstrations, portrayals of eighteenth-century residents, music performances, plays, and special tours to make your visit to Colonial Williamsburg a delight for both adults and children.

DeWitt Wallace Decorative Arts Gallery
325 Francis Street, Williamsburg (757-229-1110).

Follow the green and white Colonial Williamsburg directional signs located on all access roads in the area (exits 238A or 242A off I-64). The museum is located between South Henry and Nassau Streets, adjacent to the Restored Area of Colonial Williamsburg. It is located at Colonial Williamsburg bus stop 7.

- Open daily 10:00 a.m. to 6:00 p.m.
- Admission included for holders of Colonial Williamsburg Patriot Pass. Separate admission is $8.00. Rates are subject to change.
- Free parking in the Nassau Street parking area. However, it is much more convenient to use the Colonial Williamsburg bus and get off at stop 7.
- For 24-hour program information about exhibits, tours, and programs call (757) 220-7724. Also check the Visitor's Companion.
- Handicapped access: Parking with ramped access to the main floor of the Public Hospital through the gate at the back of the west exercise yard.
- Self-service cafe open for lunch, tea, light snacks.
- Museum shop.

The DeWitt Wallace Gallery is one of the exhibition buildings of Colonial Williamsburg. Entered through the reconstructed Public Hospital of 1773, the Wallace Gallery is a contemporary bi-level museum displaying a broad range of English and American decorative arts dating from about 1600 through 1830. Galleries include exhibits of furniture, metals, ceramics, glass, paintings, prints, maps, and textiles. Gallery exhibits are designed to expand upon the visitor's experience in the Historic Area. Older children and adults will enjoy the opportunity to compare English and colonial technologies of the eighteenth century. Be sure to visit the Lila Acheson Wallace Garden, a charming formal outdoor garden on the upper level.

There are many special events of interest to children and families scheduled in the Hennage Auditorium. Check the Visitor's Companion for scheduled events, time, and fee. The museum shop is outstanding and well worth taking the time to browse about.

Jamestown Island

Jamestown (757-229-1733).

Take I-64 to Route 199 (exit 242A). Follow Route 199 West to Colonial Parkway and follow signs to Jamestown. The Colonial Parkway is a 23-mile scenic roadway which connects Jamestown, Williamsburg, and Yorktown. There are picnic facilities available along the way.

- Open daily 9:00 a.m. to 5:30 p.m.
- $8.00 per car. Holders of Golden Age, Golden Eagle, or Golden Access passports are admitted free.
- Guided and self-guided tours.
- Theatre.
- Self-guided auto tour.
- Wheelchairs and strollers available.
- Glassmaking demonstrations.
- Pottery-making demonstrations.
- Gift shop.
- Colonial Ranger Programs for children and families.

Jamestown Island is operated by the United States Park Service. In the Visitor Center, a 15-minute film, *Jamestown—Where a Nation Began,* provides an excellent and easy-to-follow introduction to the establishment of the first English settlement in North America. There are many artifacts on exhibit that have been traced to these English settlers who arrived on three small boats. On exhibit are bowls, tools, coins, bottles, buckles, combs, and thimbles. The Visitor Center also contains many Indian artifacts of that period. There is also a model of the James Fort which has been reconstructed at nearby Jamestown Settlement. Be sure to pick up a map and information sheet before leaving the Visitor Center.

In spring, summer, and fall, Park Rangers offer regularly scheduled guided tours that last about 30 minutes. The tour begins at Monument Plaza behind the Visitor Center. Located on Jamestown Island is the historic church where the first representative assembly in the New World met in 1619. Visitors can walk the streets of old Jamestown where there are audio points to interpret the sites. The foundations of many houses and other buildings were excavated by archeologists in the 1930's and 1950's.

At the Dale House, visitors may, on a seasonal basis, watch pottery being made using seventeenth and eighteenth century designs from the Jamestown archeology collection.

The Colonial Ranger program is offered for children aged 6 through 12. The activity lasts about two hours and children work with a Park Ranger by participating in interpretive programs and completing activity sheets. Once completed, the children receive a certificate and a patch. The Rangers also conduct a 20-minute, family-oriented program which explains the life of the settlers at Jamestown. It is offered during the summer months twice a day, once in the morning and once in the afternoon.

The 3-mile and the 5-mile auto loop tour through woodland and marsh are very pleasant and allow visitors to gain a perspective of the terrain that was found by the first settlers.

Plan on spending about two hours at Jamestown Island and, if possible, see it in conjunction with Jamestown Settlement just up the road. Before leaving the island, stop at the Glasshouse and see glass being blown in the seventeenth century manner by costumed craftsmen. Some of the glass objects made here are sold to visitors. There is also a large, comprehensive gift shop in the Visitor Center.

Glassblower at
Jamestown
Island

Jamestown Settlement

Route 31 South at the Colonial Parkway, Jamestown (757-229-1607).

Take I-64 to Route 199 (exit 242A). Follow Route 199 West to Colonial Parkway and follow signs to Jamestown. The Colonial Parkway is a 23-mile scenic roadway which connects Jamestown, Williamsburg, and Yorktown. There are picnic areas along the way. Jamestown Settlement is located just 10 minutes from Colonial Williamsburg.

- Open daily 9:00 a.m. to 5:00 p.m. Closed Christmas Day and New Year's Day. The outdoor exhibits are closed in January and February.
- Adults $9.00, children (6-12) $4.25, under 6 free. A Combination Ticket is available for Jamestown Settlement and the Yorktown Victory Center. Adults $12.50, children (6-12) $6.00. All rates are subject to change.
- "Hands-on" program for 4- to 6-year-olds, first and second graders, third and fourth graders, and for parent and child. Call the Education Department at (757) 253-4939 for registration information.
- Special Event days.
- Comprehensive programs for school groups. Pre- and post-visit materials are provided for all scheduled school groups. Curriculum-based guided tours are available. Advance reservations are required. Call the Education Office at (757) 253-4939.
- Gift shop.
- Restaurant.

Jamestown, established in 1607, was the first permanent English settlement in the New World. Jamestown Settlement is a living history indoor-outdoor museum that tells its story through film, exhibition galleries, and outdoor recreated areas. Take time to see *Jamestown: The Beginning*, an excellent orientation film. The museum's galleries trace the history of England's exploration of the New World and Jamestown's beginnings to the establishment of the colony of Virginia. Using original artifacts, maps, documents, dioramas, and "hands-on" exhibits, the visitor learns who the settlers were and why they came. Visitors explore the world of the Powhatan Indian and also learn about the establishment of the colony and the legacy of Jamestown.

Outdoors, enter the recreated world of seventeenth century Virginia. There is a Powhatan Indian Village to explore and costumed interpreters to explain and answer questions about the Powhatan way of life. In the James Fort, costumed interpreters use seventeenth century skills and technology to present a living history of the daily life of the Jamestown colonists.

Replicas of the *Susan Constant*, the *Godspeed*, and the *Discovery*, the three ships that brought the English settlers in 1607, are docked on the James River. Visitors can board one of the ships and chat with a costumed "sailor" to learn more about life at sea in the seventeenth century.

During the summer, exciting "hands-on" programs are offered which are designed to enhance children's learning about Virginia's heritage. These classes are extremely popular, so do call early. Advance reservations are required. The number for the Education Office is 253-4939.

There are several special event days scattered throughout the year. In March, reenactment groups depicting soldiers from the Middle Ages to modern times demonstrate military tactics and camp life. In May, Jamestown Landing Day is commemorated with militia presentations and sailing demonstrations. June brings the Virginia Indian Heritage Festival. Old English games, puppet shows, Indian arts and crafts, nautical skills, and militia drills demonstrate seventeenth century style fun. In November, visitors can learn about seventeenth century food preservation and cooking techniques. A Jamestown Christmas illustrates traditional English Christmas celebrations and periodic music and dance performances. Call for specific dates for these events.

A very nice, large gift shop contains a wide variety of interesting items for both children and adults.

Replicas of the *Godspeed*, *Susan Constant*, and *Discovery*, the three ships that brought the colonists to Jamestown in 1607.

Muscarelle Museum of Art

College of William and Mary, Williamsburg (757-221-2700).

Take I-64 to Route 199 (exit 242A). Follow Route 199 West to Jamestown Road. Right on Jamestown Road to College. The museum is located on the left adjacent to Phi Beta Kappa Hall.

- Open Monday to Friday, 10:00 a.m. to 4:45 p.m. Saturday and Sunday, 12:00 noon to 4:00 p.m.
- Free admission.
- Free parking.
- Handicapped accessible. Elevator to second floor.
- Free guided tours. Call (757) 221-2700 for reservations.
- Children's classes and workshops.

This delightful art museum houses an impressive collection of both permanent and changing exhibits. Of special interest to children are the wide variety of classes and workshops offered. The Gallery/Studio program offers classes three times a year—fall, spring, and summer—for preschoolers with parents, up through ninth graders. Each session consists of eight classes which meet Saturdays during the fall and spring, and on Tuesdays and Thursdays during the month of July. The program combines gallery discussions about works of art on display with informal, creative, studio sessions. Spaces are limited. Call the Education Office (757-221-2703) for additional information. The museum also sponsors a number of art workshops focusing on a particular theme for students ranging in age from kindergarten through the ninth grade.

Trying on armor in Jamestown Settlement's recreated fort. *Courtesy of the Jamestown/ Yorktown Foundation.*

In addition, the museum participates in a joint program with James City County Parks and Recreation and offers Specialty Camps for children ages 7 to 15. The camps focus on a variety of themes such as archeology, theater, art, and environmental education. Registration is at the James City/Williamsburg Recreation Center.

On-the-Hill

121 Alexander Hamilton Blvd., Yorktown (757-898-3076).

Take I-64 to Yorktown exit (242B). Follow Route 199 East to Colonial Parkway and follow signs to Yorktown. Or take I-64 to Ft. Eustis Blvd. east exit (250B). Turn left on George Washington Memorial Highway (Route 17) to Alexander Hamilton Blvd.

- Open Tuesday through Saturday, 10:00 a.m. to 5:00 p.m. Sunday, 12:00 noon to 5:00 p.m.
- Free admission.
- Group tours available.
- Workshops for children.

Sponsored by the Yorktown Arts Foundation, the art gallery offers fine arts and crafts for sale. On exhibit are current works of over 30 artists and artisans in 22 media. Live demonstrations can be seen and art workshops for adults and children are offered. Call for dates, times, and cost.

Waterman's Museum

309 Water Street, Yorktown (757-887-2641).

Take I-64 to Yorktown exit (242B). Follow signs on the Colonial Parkway to Yorktown. Or take I-64 to Ft. Eustis Blvd. east exit (250B). Turn left on George Washington Memorial Highway (Route 17) and follow into Yorktown. The Museum is located on the Yorktown waterfront.

- Open April 1 to December 15. Tuesday to Saturday, 10:00 a.m. to 4:00 p.m. Sunday, 1:00 p.m. to 4:00 p.m. Closed Mondays (except Monday holidays).
- Adults $2.50, children (over 6) 50 cents, active military and senior citizens 75 cents. All rates are subject to change.
- "Hands-on" tours.
- Group tours.

- Free parking.
- Handicapped accessible.
- Gift shop.
- Cruises. Rates are subject to change.
- Picnic tables nearby.

The term "waterman" is used exclusively for fishermen on the Thames River in London, England, and for fishermen on the Chesapeake Bay. The term means "those who work the water year round." The museum tells the story of the Virginia watermen and their boats—what they do and how they make their living. The Native American Indians were the first watermen to work the waters of the Chesapeake Bay and its tributaries and taught their methods to the early settlers. Visitors also learn about present-day methods used by watermen for crabbing, clamming, oystering, eel fishing, and pound net fishing. Did you know that scallops are the only bivalve to have a patron saint? Another gallery presents an exhibit of boats and early instruments. There is a 4-minute video that examines fishing and clamming and explains how the catch is prepared for market. Another gallery features "hands-on" opportunities where visitors can touch, examine, and identify shells. Throughout the museum, there is an emphasis on Bay ecology and the animals of the Bay.

The museum itself is housed in the old Cypress Manor built in 1935-36 by Benjamin Fernald and brought upriver to its present site in Yorktown.

Outdoors, there is a deadrise work boat, a 100-year-old log canoe, and other exhibits. Parents may arrange for small groups of young visitors to have a "hands-on" experience. Youngsters can try tonging for oysters and collect and identify specimens found on the beach. The museum is staffed mainly by volunteers, so call for reservations to be certain a volunteer will be available. An interesting gift shop is located in a separate building on the site with many items priced to accommodate a child's allowance.

During the summer months, take a cruise down the York River. The 16-passenger *Erin Kay* leaves the museum dock Thursday to Sunday at 5:00 p.m. and returns at 6:30 p.m. There is an additional cruise at 3:00 p.m. on Fridays and Sundays. An interpreter is aboard who talks about the river and the shoreline during the 1 1/2-hour cruise. Tickets are $10.00 per person, $5.00 for children under 12, and free for those 6 and under. Tickets are available at the dock gate about an hour before each departure.

Yorktown Victory Center

Yorktown (757-887-1776).

Take I-64 to Yorktown exit (242B). Follow Route 199 East to Colonial Parkway and follow signs to Yorktown. The Colonial Parkway is a 23-mile scenic roadway which connects Yorktown, Williamsburg, and Jamestown. There are picnic facilities available at the Ringfield and Great Neck picnic areas. Or take I-64 to Ft. Eustis Blvd. east exit (250B). Turn left on George Washington Memorial Highway (Route 17) and continue to Yorktown. The Victory Center is located on the edge of town on Route 1060 off Routes 238 and 17.

- Open daily 9:00 a.m. to 5:00 p.m.
- Adults $6.75, children (6-12) $3.25, under 6 free. A Combination Ticket with Jamestown Settlement is available. Adults $12.50, children (6-12) $3.25. All rates are subject to change.
- Free parking.
- Workshops for children.
- Special programs and events.
- Handicapped accessible.
- Picnic facilities, vending machines.
- Gift shop.

The museum's indoor galleries focus on the many stories of the American struggle for independence. The six galleries enhance the visitor's understanding of the important role played by Yorktown in the formation of the nation. The "Witness to Revolution"

Military drill at the Continental Army Encampment, Yorktown Victory Center. *Courtesy of the Jamestown/Yorktown Foundation.*

gallery presents the stories of a diverse group of 10 people whose lives were affected by the American Revolution. Using actual diaries and correspondence, life-sized figures of ordinary men and women express their views of the conflict. Follow the ramp to the "Converging on Yorktown" gallery and learn through maps, documents, and artifacts the story of Yorktown and how it become the setting for the decisive battle of the Revolution. A new 18-minute film in gallery 3 depicts a nighttime encampment during the siege of Yorktown. Artifacts recovered during the underwater excavations of the British supply ship *Betsy* as well as a fascinating video which chronicles the excavations are shown in the "Yorktown's Sunken Fleet" gallery. "The Unfinished Revolution" exhibit in gallery 5 describes the steps that led to the adoption of the federal Constitution and the Bill of Rights. Gallery 6 houses temporary exhibitions relating to the Revolutionary War period.

Plan some time for a visit to the "Children's Kaleidoscope" Discovery Room. Your children will want to try on the colonial clothing. There is also a fully equipped, six-man military tent to examine. Have the kids put their hands in the "surprise boxes" and see if they can guess what's inside. They will also discover that writing with a quill pen is quite different from writing with a ball point pen. Afterwards, they can take a penmanship book home with them. It will make a wonderful souvenir of their visit to Yorktown. The Discovery Room is open weekends during the school year and daily during the summer.

Outdoors, there is the Continental Army Encampment. Costumed interpreters recreate a Continental Army camp. Visitors can discuss the daily life of the soldier and his family with the interpreters. Do encourage your children to ask questions.

Also outdoors is the eighteenth-century farm site. Crop fields and vegetable garden, a tobacco barn, and a log kitchen depict rural life on a typical small farm. Costumed interpreters demonstrate daily and seasonal activities of farm life of the period.

There are many "hands-on" programs available that have been designed to make learning about Virginia's heritage fun and exciting for children. The programs are offered throughout the summer. The "Young Patriots" is for 4 to 6 year-olds, first and second graders can participate in the "Young Colonials" program, and the "Young Continentals" program is for third and fourth graders. These classes are very popular and fill up quickly. Call the Education Office at (757) 253-4939 to make the required reservations. Classroom enrichment programs are available and advance reservations are required. Call (757) 253-4939. The programs are adaptable for early elementary grades through twelfth grade.

Throughout the year, there are a number of special events. In June "The Yorktown Sampler" is held. This is a family-centered festival that provides a view of domestic life and colonial culture through "hands-on" programs and activities for all ages. "The Children's Colonial Days Fair" takes place in July. Children are invited to play traditional games, compete in contests, and make crafts to take home. "Yorktown Day Weekend" in October is part of a town-wide observance of Washington's victory at Yorktown on October 19, 1781. September brings the "Holiday Crafts Workshop." Families are invited to make seasonal decorations and craft projects. Also in December is the Annual Tree Lighting. Families may celebrate the holiday season with music, story-telling, Santa Claus, and the illumination of a large evergreen tree. Call (757) 887-1776 for specific dates and times for events.

A very nice gift shop with many items for children is located in the Center.

Yorktown Visitor Center and Battlefields
Yorktown (757-898-3400).

Take I-64 to Yorktown exit (242B). Follow Route 199 East to Colonial Parkway and follow signs to Yorktown Visitor Center. The Colonial Parkway is a 23-mile scenic roadway which connects Yorktown, Williamsburg, and Jamestown. There are picnic facilities available at the Great Neck picnic area. Or take I-64 to Ft. Eustis Blvd. east exit (250B). Turn left on George Washington Memorial Highway (Route 17) and follow signs to the Visitor Center.

- Open daily 8:30 a.m. to 5:30 p.m.
- Free admission.
- Free parking.
- Handicapped accessible. Wheelchairs available. Tape recordings for the blind.
- Free guided walking tour.
- Colonial Ranger program.
- Special classroom enrichment programs.
- Gift shop.

Operated by the National Park Service, the Yorktown Visitor Center invites visitors to see a 16-minute orientation film describing the Battle of Yorktown and the historic surrender. In the exhibit area, visitors may explore a full-sized reconstruction of a British frigate of the 1780's. Also on display is one of George

Washington's original field tents used during the siege of Yorktown. Here is one place where Washington really did sleep. Visitors can see relics found in the York River. These objects from British ships had rested in the mud of the York River for 150 years. Children will enjoy seeing the Augustine Moore House in miniature. This dollhouse-like structure is fully furnished down to the last detail and is a delight to see. At the rear of the Visitor Center, step outdoors to the large observation deck that overlooks the battlefields.

Before leaving the Visitor Center, check the board for the times the next Ranger-conducted walking tour takes place. The very informative tour lasts between 30 and 40 minutes. Also be sure to pick up a map of the town as well as a map to serve as a guide for the 7-mile, self-guided auto battlefield tour and the 9-mile, self-guided auto siege encampment tour of the 1781 battle. A cassette player and auto tape tour is available for rent for $2.00 in the gift shop.

After leaving the Visitor Center, head into town and take the 45-minute walking tour around this charming, historic town. Be sure to visit the home of Thomas Nelson, Jr., one of the signers of the Declaration of Independence (see the Thomas Nelson, Jr. House, page 46). Using the map obtained at the Visitor Center, explore the waterfront, historic Grace Episcopal Church and graveyard, the Drum Museum, and the shops. Return to your car and enjoy a leisurely drive on the self-guided battlefield and encampment tours.

The Colonial Ranger Program is offered for children aged 6 through 12. The activity lasts about 2 hours and children work with a Park Ranger by participating in interpretive programs and completing activity sheets. Once completed, the children receive a certificate and a patch.

Programs for school groups that last approximately 1 hour are also conducted by the Park Rangers and are adaptable for first through twelfth graders. Pre-visit materials are sent upon reservation confirmation. For reservations and further information call (757) 898-3400.

Yorktown Day is celebrated every year to commemorate the historic victory and the signing of the Treaty of Paris. The Fife and Drum Corps play, there's a wonderful parade to watch, speeches to hear, and the marching bands of the military services to entertain. Lunch is available at Grace Episcopal Church.

During the summer, every Tuesday evening at 7:30, the Fife and Drums Corps of Yorktown performs a 20-minute program at the Victory Monument.

Hampton

Air Power Park

413 West Mercury Blvd., Hampton (757-727-1163).

From I-64 take Mercury Blvd. exit (263B). Follow Mercury Blvd. north approximately 2 miles to the Park on the right.

- Open daily 9:30 a.m. to 4:30 p.m.
- Free admission.
- Free parking.
- Air- and space-related outdoor playground.

Young pilot and astronaut "wannabes" will enjoy this unusual air park. Many models of aircraft are on display inside the museum. Children can pretend to be flying an airplane by just pushing a button to operate the "hands-on" wind tunnel.

Outdoors, there are real airplanes, rockets, and other aircraft. Of special interest is the unusual playground. The equipment in this play area consists of replicas of air and space vehicles. For example, the three-story slide looks like a rocket, the monkey bars resemble space capsules, and the double-seated "airplane" bounces up and down. There are also bouncing jets to ride.

For those wishing to pack a lunch, picnic tables are provided. Located not too far from Coliseum Mall, the Park is a good place to let kids unwind after shopping.

Aerial view of Air Power Park, Hampton. *Courtesy of Hampton Conventions and Tourism.*

Casemate Museum

Fort Monroe, Hampton (757-727-3391).

Take I-64 to Mercury Blvd. exit (263B). Follow Mercury Blvd. north about 3 3/4 miles to the entrance to Ft. Monroe. Follow signs to the Museum.

- Open daily 10:30 a.m. to 4:30 p.m. Closed Thanksgiving, Christmas, and New Year's Day.
- Free admission.
- Free parking.
- Gift shop.
- Buffet lunch and dinner is offered at the adjacent Chamberlin Hotel.

The Casemate Museum is located at Fort Monroe which is the headquarters for the United States Army Training and Doctrine Command (TRADOC). It contains the largest stone fort ever built by the United States and the only moat-encircled fort still used by the Army.

A casemate is a chamber in a wall of a fort which can be used as a gun position or as storage or living quarters. On display in the museum is the cell in which Confederate President Jefferson Davis was imprisoned after the Civil War. On exhibit are hand weapons, uniforms, models, and drawings dating from the Civil War. Edgar Allan Poe, at the time an Army sergeant, was stationed at Fort Monroe for a short period prior to his appointment to West Point. There are many guns, cannons and Civil War memorabilia on exhibit as well as an interesting film.

The museum is the starting point for a walking tour that takes the visitor past Robert E. Lee's quarters, the famous Lincoln gun, an

Firing the cannon at Casemate Museum, Hampton.

old chapel, and the beautiful Chamberlin Hotel located on the water. Families will enjoy the buffet lunch and dinner offered in the hotel's dining room that has a view of the water. The hotel is surrounded by a park with a gazebo that houses band concerts. In the summertime, concerts are performed by the TRADOC band on Thursday nights at 7:30 in the park. There is also a walking and jogging trail along the water.

Hampton University Museum
Academy Building, Hampton University, Hampton (757-727-5308).

Take I-64 to County Street exit (267). Cross Settlers Landing Road and proceed straight to the University on the left. Follow the signs to the Museum.

- Open daily except holidays and campus holidays, 8.00 a.m. to 5:00 p.m. Saturday and Sunday, noon to 4:00 p.m.
- Free admission
- Free parking.
- Gift shop.

The Museum is located on the beautiful campus of Hampton University and is housed in the Academy Building, a National Historic Landmark. The University was founded in 1868 for the education of newly freed African-Americans. The Museum contains an African collection of nearly 2700 pieces representing 87 ethnic groups and cultures. The American Indian collection contains 1600 pieces from 93 tribes. The Fine Art collection contains over 1200 works in a variety of media, including paintings, graphics, and sculptures. There are also some very fine pieces in the Asian and Oceanic collection. The Museum is recommended for older children or high school students.

Virginia Air & Space Center and Hampton Roads History Center
600 Settlers Landing Road, Hampton
(757-727-0900 or 1-800-296-0800).

Take I-64 to exit 267. Right on Settlers Landing Road. Cross over the bridge to the Center on the left.

- Open daily 9:00 a.m. to 5:00 p.m.
- Adults $6.00, children (3-11) $4.00. IMAX Theater: adults $5.50, children $4.50. Discount available for combination tickets. All rates are subject to change.
- Parking garage directly across street from Center.
- IMAX Theater.
- Observation deck.

- "Hands-on" exhibits.
- Handicapped accessible.
- Gift shop.

The Air & Space Center, housed in a modern structure towering as high as nine stories in some places, is one of the area's new museums. It features exhibits which run the gamut from early flights to aerospace technology. It contains a Science Center, History Corner, and Space Gallery. While many museums focus on their respective collections, the Center focuses on education. Many "hands-on" exhibits and special programs are available for all ages.

The Center's collections include the Apollo 12 Command Module, the Mercury 14 F-4E "Phantom II," the USS Yorktown model, and numerous air and space craft that appear to float from the Center's soaring 94-foot ceiling.

Other Center highlights include a variety of kid-tested and family-approved "hands-on" exhibits. Exhibits such as the Planet Juro Motion Simulator, Astronaut-for-a-Minute, and Launch-a-Rocket allow visitors to watch videos, make timely decisions, and push buttons. An observation deck is located on the upper level. Not to be missed is the 300-seat IMAX Theater, which features a giant five-part projection screen and 16,000 watts of electrifying sound and is a "must" for both children and adults.

Before or after the visit to the Center, be sure to pay a visit to the Hampton Carousel located right next to the Center (see listing under Hampton Carousel, page 49). Or make a day of it and combine a visit to the Center with a boat ride leaving from the Hampton Visitor Center right down the street (see listing under Harbor Cruises, page 56).

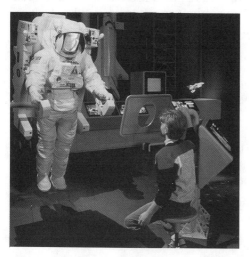

An Astronaut's space suit at the Virginia Air & Space Center. *Courtesy of the Virginia Air & Space Center.*

Newport News

The Mariners' Museum

100 Museum Drive, Newport News
(757-596-2222 or 1-800-591-SAIL).

Take I-64 to J. Clyde Morris Blvd. exit (258A) and follow Route 17 South approximately 3 miles to the entrance of the Museum.

- Open daily 10:00 a.m. to 5:00 p.m.
- Adults $6.00, children (6-12) $3.25, under 6 are free.
  Rates are subject to change.
- Free parking
- Free guided tours.
- Hiking trail and picnic facilities.
- Research library.
- Museum shop.

The Mariners' Museum contains a renowned collection of hand-crafted ship models, small craft from around the world, navigation instruments, and priceless artifacts found in old ships. Canoes, row boats, sail boats, power boats, and racing boats are on display. Visitors can learn about fishing in the Chesapeake Bay and trace the growth of the largest naval complex in the world.

A lighthouse that actually turns, a working steam engine, and a buoy are displayed. The Museum houses the finest collection of ship figureheads in the United States.

The Crabtree Gallery features 16 miniature, handcrafted-to-scale vessels. They range from a primitive raft to an exquisitely decorated Venetian galley, all hand-carved over several decades by artist August Crabtree. Each model is crafted from exotic woods and depicts a different era in water transportation.

There are several "hands-on" activities that children will enjoy. They can touch a crabbing skiff, test their skill at knot tying, and play a video computer game on water safety and navigation. The film *Mariners* is shown in the theatre.

The research library is open all year and is an assisted library open to the public. The Gift Gallery features unique maritime items as well as inexpensive gifts suitable for children.

Outdoors, families may enjoy a picnic in Mariners' Museum Park, and fish or boat in the lake. (See pages 71 to 74 for additional information.)

Peninsula Fine Arts Gallery

101 Museum Drive, Newport News (757-596-8175).

Take I-64 to J. Clyde Morris Blvd. exit (258A). Follow J. Clyde Morris Blvd. (Route 17) south to Warwick Blvd. (Route 60), approximately 2 1/2 miles to entrance of Peninsula Fine Arts Museum and Mariners' Museum.

- Free admission.
- Open Tuesday to Saturday, 10:00 a.m. to 5:00 p.m. Sunday, 1:00 p.m. to 5:00 p.m. Closed Monday.
- Free parking
- Classes, workshops, and special events. Call 596-8175 for additional information.
- Gift shop.

The Peninsula Fine Arts Gallery, an affiliate of the Virginia Museum, is located next door to the Mariners' Museum in Huntington Park. The Gallery contains fascinating works of art in several styles and media, including photography, oils, prints, and sculptures. Much of the collection changes seasonally. The Gallery features a unique collection of Tiffany glass.

A large gift shop adjacent to the museum contains many lovely and unusual items for both children and adults.

The United States Army Transportation Museum

Building 300, Besson Hall, Fort Eustis, Newport News (757-878-1182/1183).

Take I-64 to Ft. Eustis Blvd. west exit (250A) and continue straight 1 mile to sentry gate. Both military and civilians are admitted.

- Open daily 9:00 a.m. to 4:30 p.m. Open Memorial Day, Fourth of July, and Labor Day. Closed federal holidays and Easter Sunday.
- Free admission.
- Free parking.
- Handicapped accessible.
- Gift shop.
- Group tours available by appointment. Call (757) 878-1183.

The Museum features both indoor and outdoor exhibits. Stop in the theatre and see a film on the history of the Army Transportation Corps. The indoor exhibits present a history of the world of motion including rail, land, air, and sea, using miniature models, dioramas and life-sized displays. On view is the first helicopter to land at the South Pole and a vertical take-off and landing aircraft. Also exhibited is the experimental Delachner Aerocycle—a rocket belt designed to carry one soldier on short, low-level flights. There is the opportunity to learn about the movement of soldiers and equipment in war and peace, from the "Red Ball Express" of World War II, to the armored vehicles used in the jungles of Vietnam, to the "flying jeeps" of today.

The outdoor Marine Park and Aircraft Pavilion provides a wonderful opportunity for children to see actual trucks, landing craft, planes, helicopters, and engines. Located on the opposite side of the museum is the very interesting rail exhibit.

The gift shop contains army memorabilia, toys, and models of various modes of transportation.

Virginia Living Museum

524 J. Clyde Morris Blvd., Newport News (757-595-1900).

Take I-64 to J. Clyde Morris Blvd. west exit (258A) and continue 2 miles to museum on left.

- Open daily year round.

Museum/Observatory:

- Summer hours (Memorial Day to Labor Day): Monday to Saturday, 9:00 a.m. to 6:00 p.m. Open to 9:00 p.m. Thursdays. Sunday, 10:00 a.m. to 6:00 p.m.
- Winter hours (Labor Day to Memorial Day): Monday to Saturday, 9:00 a.m. to 5:00 p.m. Sunday, 12:00 p.m. to 5:00 p.m. Closed Thanksgiving Day, Christmas Eve, Christmas Day, New Year's Day.
- Adults $5.00, children (3-12) $3.25. Children under 3 are admitted free.

Planetarium Shows:

- Summer hours: Monday to Sunday, 11:00 a.m., 1:30 p.m., 2:30 p.m., 3:30 p.m. Thursday evening, 8:00 p.m.
- Winter hours: Monday to Friday, 3:30 p.m. Saturday, 11:00 a.m., 1:30 p.m., 2:30 p.m., 3:30 p.m. Sunday, 1:30 p.m., 2:30 p.m., 3:30 p.m. Thursday evening, 7:30 p.m.
- Adults $2.50, children (3-12) $2.00.

Combination ticket:

Adults $6.00, children (3-12) $4.00. Children under 4 are not admitted to the Planetarium.

- All rates are subject to change.
- Birthday parties.
- Outreach programs.
- Special school programs and group rates.
- Free parking.
- Entire facility is wheelchair accessible.
- Gift shop.

Children of all ages will enjoy this combination science museum, wildlife park, aquarium, botanical preserve, and planetarium. An outdoor aviary focuses on the importance of wetlands, birds, and other creatures that inhabit bog, marsh, and swamp ecosystems. During the spring and summer seasons, be sure to visit the newly built outdoor butterfly garden which contains a variety of plants that attract many species of butterflies.

The indoor exhibits begin with a 60-foot cross-section of the James River showing life in a mountain stream and ending with life in the Atlantic Ocean. At the Touch Tank, children can experience a supervised "hands-on" meeting with nature. A volunteer is there to assist in handling sea stars, hermit crabs, anenomes, horseshoe crabs, and snails, and also to answer questions. There are steps and platforms that permit easy viewing for visitors of all heights in the fascinating "How Life Survives" exhibit. In the Discovery Center, children have the opportunity for additional supervised "hands-on" experiences. There are objects to touch, questions to answer, as well as slides to examine under microscopes. The Observatory contains a 14-inch telescope and there is a volunteer present to explain how to use it. Visitors may browse about inside a two-story aviary that features beautiful songbirds in a natural habitat. Next to the aviary, on the lower level, is the "World of Darkness" exhibit which houses an intriguing array of nocturnal creatures such as flying squirrels and bats.

Outdoors, enjoy a wonderful stroll on a picturesque boardwalk. This walkway meanders along Deer Creek and permits close-up views of native water animals. Raccoon, beaver, fox, bobcat, deer, wild turkey, skunk, and two bald eagles come into view. Benches scattered along the way invite visitors to linger and enjoy nature.

The Planetarium is a state-of-the-art theatre and is well known for its creative and informative shows.

The Museum sponsors workshops and classes for young naturalists from kindergarten through fifth grade. The Explorer Series is for grades 6 to 8. There are "Weekend Safaris" for the whole family. Adult education courses are also given. Call (757) 595-1900 for additional information.

An Outreach Program presents educational programs on a weekly or monthly basis for groups. The programs last 40 minutes and demonstrate live animals. Call (757) 595-1900 for additional information.

A decorated room and a 10-minute live animal show is available for birthday parties and includes admission to all indoor and outdoor natural history exhibits. Call the reservations coordinator at (757) 595-1900 for additional information.

Summer Field Schools are offered to sixth graders. This is a week-long trip to the Outer Banks of North Carolina. Call the museum for further information.

War Memorial Museum of Virginia

9285 Warwick Blvd. Huntington Park, Newport News (757-247-8523)

Take I-64 to Mercury Blvd./James River exit (263A). Follow Mercury Blvd. (Route 258) to Warwick Blvd. (Route 60) and turn right. The museum is located just west of the YMCA and is surrounded by Huntington Park.

- Open daily 9:00 a.m. to 5:00 p.m. Closed Thanksgiving, Christmas Day, New Year's Day.
- Adults $2.00, children and senior citizens $1.00. Half price for active military. Rates are subject to change.
- Free parking.
- Weekend films. Call (757) 247-8523 for show and times.
- Gift shop.
- Educational programs. Workshops for students and teachers. Call (757) 247-8523 for additional information.
- Picnic areas in Huntington Park.

The War Memorial Museum offers its visitors a visual experience in military history from 1775 to the present. Over 50,000 artifacts are on display. Military vehicles relating to every major United States military involvement can be seen. There are displays of guns and weapons, uniforms, and propaganda posters. There are sections covering the black soldier and other sections depicting women at war. Also on display are exhibits from Italy, Germany, and Japan during World Wars I and II. Military history films are shown every weekend and are included in the price of admission. Before leaving the museum, do make a stop in the rest rooms for a surprise. You will be glad you did.

The Educational Department provides assistance for teachers to develop a visit appropriate for any age group. Student workshops run the gamut from the Revolutionary War soldier's life to the seeds of dictatorship, to Vietnam revisited. Movies, multi-media presentations, focus tours, and "hands-on" activities are available.

Outdoors, families can enjoy the picnic areas and recreational facilities of Huntington Park (see listing under Huntington Park on page 72).

Plantations and Historic Houses

Mention historic houses and antique furniture to most kids, and they ask, "When can we go to Busch Gardens?"

Still, there is much to capture their interest once you get them there. A visit to a plantation means that children can actually see and explore some of the places they read about in their social studies books. Before they know it, they have forgotten all about the theme park and instead are lost in fascination over the slave quarters or some other facet of plantation life.

A relatively short drive will enable them to visit some of the actual sites where our nation's history began. We have alphabetically listed several of the magnificent plantations and historic homes that played an important role in America's early history.

Please remember when planning an outing of this type that touring should be limited to one or two plantations per day. Make a day of it and bring a picnic lunch along or plan to include a stop at an interesting restaurant (see "Restaurants", page 120, for suggestions).

Berkeley Plantation

Route 5, Charles City (757-829-6018).

Located 26 miles west of Williamsburg on historic State Route 5.

- Open daily 8:00 a.m. to 5:00 p.m. Closed Christmas Day.
- Adults $8.50, children (6-16) $4.25. All rates are subject to change. Block tickets are available for $25.00 and include Berkeley, Shirley, Evelynton, and Sherwood Forest Plantations.
- Ancestral home of the Harrisons—two Presidents and a signer of the Declaration of Independence.
- Site of America's first Thanksgiving.
- Site where "Taps" was composed.
- Coach House Tavern.
- Gift shop.

Built in 1726, this early Georgian brick mansion is the first house in Virginia built with a pediment roof. The mansion is situated on a beautifully landscaped hilltop overlooking the James River. Ten acres of formal boxwood gardens and lawns extend a full quarter mile from the front door to the river.

Benjamin Harrison, son of the builder of Berkeley, was a signer of the Declaration of Independence. His third son, William Henry Harrison, was the ninth President of the United States. His grandson was Benjamin Harrison, twenty-third President of the United States.

The windows, floors, and pediment roof are all original. The remainder of the mansion has been beautifully restored. The rooms are furnished with antiques authentic to the period with several coming from nearby Westover Plantation. A costumed interpreter conducts a well-presented and fascinating tour of the first floor of the mansion.

The tour begins in the basement where visitors watch a 10-minute orientation slide program as well as view several interesting exhibits and paintings. The Plantation was occupied by General McClellan and the Army of the Potomac during the Civil War and was visited by President Lincoln. The father of the present owner, Malcolm Jamieson, served with McClellan as drummer boy.

Enjoy a stroll through the beautifully landscaped grounds and boxwood gardens down to the banks of the James River. Follow

Manor House at Berkeley Plantation, Charles City. *Courtesy of Berkeley Plantation.*

the path that leads to the site where "Taps" was composed in 1862 and also to the Harrison family graveyard.

The first American Thanksgiving took place at Berkeley in 1619. This day is recreated yearly on the first Sunday in November. Visitors have the opportunity to be part of this recreation of history. It is a wonderful outing for the whole family. For detailed information write Virginia Thanksgiving Festival, Inc., P.O.Box 5132, Richmond, VA 23220, or call (757) 272-3226. In conjunction with the recreation, the Berkeley Thanksgiving Festival also sponsors an essay contest. Virginia fourth graders are invited to submit essays and the best winning essay is reprinted in the program. Ten other award winners also receive United States Savings Bonds.

The outstanding Coach House Tavern is open daily for lunch. Reservations are required for dinner. Call (757) 829-6003.

Carter's Grove

Route 60 East, Williamsburg (757-229-1000).

Follow the green and white Colonial Williamsburg directional signs located on all access roads in the area (exits 238A or 242A off I-64) to the Visitor's Center. Carter's Grove is located 8 miles east of Colonial Williamsburg and can only be reached by auto. Follow Route 60 East to Carter's Grove on the right. Return via The Old Country Road, a private, one-way lane.

- Open daily, mid-March through the first Sunday in October, 9:00 a.m. to 5:00 p.m. Open daily, November and December, 9:00 a.m. to 4:00 p.m. Closed last week of November for installation of Christmas decorations. Closed January to mid-March.
- Admission included with Colonial Williamsburg Patriot Pass (see listing under Colonial Williamsburg, page 14). Separate admission tickets may be purchased at Carter's Grove reception area or at the Colonial Williamsburg Visitor Center. Adults $15.00, children (6-12) $9.00.
- Free parking.
- Handicapped accessible.
- Archeology museum.
- Wolstenholme Town.
- Slave Quarters Interpretive Program.

- Vending machines for snacks and drinks. Light refreshments are available at the stable.
- Gift shop.

There is much to see at Carter's Grove, so plan on at least 2 to 3 hours to visit the site. A visit to the plantation brings alive 400 years of history. Children and adults can learn about a seventeenth-century settlement, an eighteenth-century plantation, slavery, archeology, agriculture, architecture, and twentieth-century entertaining on a grand scale all in one beautiful location. An excellent 14-minute slide program in the reception area titled *A Thing Called Time*, serves as an introduction to Carter's Grove. The plantation is made up of component parts that piece together its 400-year-old history. The newly opened Winthrop Rockefeller Archeology Museum contains artifacts excavated on the site that tells the story of Martin's Hundred and Wolstenholme Town. At the Wolstenholme site, the partial reconstruction of the palisades, buildings, and fences of the seventeenth-century settlement is described by audiotapes in "talking barrels" scattered around the site.

Costumed interpreters guide the visitor through buildings and outdoor spaces of the reconstructed slave quarter. Here visitors can learn about the lives of the slaves whose labors supported the eighteenth-century plantation and about the customs and mores of slave life. Families can participate by sawing wood, pounding corn, or preparing wild game for cooking.

Tours of the mansion itself begin at the stable on the land side (or back) of the mansion. Interpreters describe life at the mansion during the 1930's when it was owned by the McCreas and the eighteenth-century heritage of ideas and styles that influenced that life. The tour takes approximately 45 minutes.

Also to be seen at Carter's Grove is the English garden that is located on the river side (or front side) of the mansion. Adjacent to the slave quarter are several fields planted with types of eighteenth-century crops. Look for livestock from Colonial Williamsburg's rare breed program in the fenced orchard.

A very nice gift shop contains many interesting items for both children and adults.

It is strongly recommended that visitors take the time to return from Carter's Grove by way of The Old Country Road. Meandering through woodlands and across tidal creeks, the road offers the visitor an excellent perspective on the terrain of Tidewater Virginia in the eighteenth century.

Evelynton Plantation

6701 John Tyler Highway, Charles City
(757-829-5075 or 1-800-473-5075).

Located approximately 25 miles west of Williamsburg on historic State Route 5.

- Open daily 9:00 a.m. to 5:00 p.m. Closed Christmas Day, New Year's Day, and Thanksgiving Day. (Call ahead weekends. Mansion may close at 3 o'clock for scheduled weddings or receptions.)
- Adults $7.00, children (6-12) $3.50, under 6 free. All rates are subject to change. Block tickets are available for $25.50 and include Evelynton, Berkeley, Shirley, and Sherwood Forest Plantations.
- Guided tour of house and grounds.
- Gift shop.

Evelynton Plantation is a part of the original land grant of 1619 to William Byrd of Westover Plantation and is named for his daughter, Evelyn Byrd. Since 1847, it has been the home of the Ruffin family (Edmund Ruffin's great-great-grandson occupies the second floor of the Georgian Revival home today).

Evelynton was the site of Civil War skirmishes in 1862 when General George McClellan waged his campaign. J.E.B. Stuart, Stonewall Jackson, and John Pelham led the Southern offensive in the battle of Evelynton Heights.

A guided tour lasting between 30 and 40 minutes details the history, occupants and furnishings of the mansion. It is listed in the National Register of Historic Places. The 60-acre grounds are beautiful and contain swings, a hammock, and picnic tables.

Moore House

Yorktown (757-898-3400).

Take I-64 to Yorktown exit (242B). Follow Route 199 East to the Colonial Parkway. The Colonial Parkway is a 23-mile scenic roadway that connects Yorktown, Williamsburg, and Jamestown. Or take I-64 to Ft. Eustis Blvd. east exit (250B). Turn left on George Washington Memorial Highway (Route 17) and continue to Yorktown Visitor Center. Stop at the Center for map and directions.

- Open daily in summer, 10:00 a.m. to 5:00 p.m. Limited viewing in winter. Call (804) 898-3400 for hours. Ask for extension 58 for interpretive recording.
- Free admission. Stop at the Visitor Center for map and information.
- Free parking.
- First floor is accessible for wheelchairs.
- Site where Articles of Capitulation were drafted.

The home, located on the York River, was built about 1735 by Augustine Moore, a merchant of Yorktown. In 1930, a $30,000 grant from the John D. Rockefeller Foundation funded the restoration of the home.

The terms of General Cornwallis' surrender to General Washington were drafted here after the siege of Yorktown. Emissaries of both camps met in the parlor of the Moore House on October 18, 1781 and drafted the Articles of Capitulation. The site is operated by the U.S. Park Service. An introduction to the history of the period and the house is conducted outdoors and then visitors are invited inside to tour the home accompanied by a living history performer.

The stone house kitchen located on the property is built on its original foundation as is the ice house.

Moore House, where the surrender terms of the Revolutionary War were negotiated, Yorktown. *Courtesy of the National Park Service, Colonial National Historic Park.*

Nelson House

Main Street, Yorktown (757-898-3400).

Take I-64 to Yorktown exit (242B). Follow Route 199 East to the Colonial Parkway and follow signs to Yorktown. The Colonial Parkway is a 23-mile scenic roadway that connects Yorktown, Williamsburg, and Jamestown. Or take I-64 to Ft. Eustis Blvd. east exit (250B). Turn left on George Washington Memorial Highway (Route 17) to either Main Street or the Yorktown Visitor Center.

- Open daily Memorial Day to Labor Day, 10:00 a.m. to 4:00 p.m. Call (757) 898-3400 for hours during the remainder of the year. Ask for extension 58 for interpretive recording. Closed Christmas Day and New Year's Day.
- Free admission.
- Free parking.
- Interpretive programs.
- "Hands-on" room.
- No handicapped accessibility.
- Stop at the Yorktown Visitor Center for map and information.

The Georgian brick home was built by "Scotch Tom" Nelson in the early 1700's and passed down to his grandson, Thomas Nelson, Jr. The house is historically significant as Thomas Nelson, Jr. was one of the signers of the Declaration of Independence. He was also the wartime Governor of Virginia and commanded the Virginia militia during the siege of Yorktown.

During the summer, there is an interpretive program performed by costumed character actors who assume the roles of Thomas Nelson, Jr. and his wife, Lucy. Performances begin promptly every half-hour every afternoon.

One of the rooms in the mansion has been reserved as a "hands-on" room. Here children will find a few colonial toys, dried herbs, a twist of tobacco, and a spinning wheel. They can also have a photo session outdoors while wearing colonial clothing.

Outdoors, there is a lovely formal English garden. Be sure to have the children find the cannonballs imbedded in the side of the house facing Nelson Street. (The cannonballs were actually placed there by a twentieth-century owner of the property.)

Sherwood Forest Plantation

Route 5, Charles City (757-829-5377).

Located 18 miles west of Williamsburg and 35 miles east of Richmond on historic State Route 5.

- Open daily 9:00 a.m. to 5:00 p.m. Closed Thanksgiving, Christmas and New Year's Day.
- Adults $7.50. Children, students, and senior citizens $4.50. Block tickets are available for $25.00 and include Sherwood Forest, Evelynton, Shirley, and Berkeley Plantations. All rates are subject to change. Call (804) 829-5377 for information.
- Home of two United States Presidents.
- Free parking.
- Handicapped accessible.
- Guided tour of house and self-guided tour of grounds.

Sherwood Forest Plantation was owned by two United States Presidents, John Tyler and William Henry Harrison. Built about 1730, it was altered and renovated by President Tyler in 1844. Since that time, the plantation has been continuously occupied by members of the Tyler family, and has been a working plantation for over 240 years. Sherwood Forest has been designated a National Historic Landmark by the U.S. Department of the Interior.

Visitors are conducted on a 30-minute guided tour of this lovely home. The grounds are beautifully landscaped with magnolias, tulip poplars, and American tree boxwood. Several of the original outbuildings (dependencies) are still standing. The Bottom Pasture, with its nineteenth-century drainage canals dug by hand-labor, is now a nature trail.

This is a lovely spot for children to be exposed to history and shake off some "car-wiggles" at the same time.

Shirley Plantation
Route 5, Charles City (1-800-232-1613).

Located approximately 35 miles west of Williamsburg on historic State Route 5.

- Open daily 9:00 a.m. to 4:30 p.m. Closed Christmas Day.
- Adults $7.50, students (13-21) $5.00, children (6-12) $3.75. Block tickets are available for $25.00 and include Shirley, Evelynton, Sherwood Forest, and Berkeley Plantations. All rates are subject to change.
- Continuous tours. Last tour begins at 4:30 p.m.
- Center of hospitality during colonial period.
- Gift shop.

Designated as a National Historic Landmark, Shirley Plantation was founded in 1613 and granted to Edward Hill in 1660. It became a center of hospitality during colonial times and many prominent Virginians, including George Washington, Thomas Jefferson, the Byrds, and the Harrisons, were lavishly entertained here.

During the American Revolution, Shirley Plantation was a supply center for the Continental Army. A century later, during the Civil War, it was used as a hospital. Ann Hill Carter, mother of Robert E. Lee, was born at Shirley Plantation.

The present mansion was begun in 1723 by the third Edward Hill for his daughter Elizabeth, who married John Carter, son of Robert "King" Carter of Carter's Grove. The home was completed in 1738 and is recognized as an architectural treasure. The famous carved walnut staircase rises three stories without any visible means of support and is the only one of its kind in America. The original floors are in remarkably good condition, and the home is filled with original furnishings, crested silver, and family portraits.

Brick out buildings form a unique Queen Anne-style court, the only standing example of this building method in the United States. The Hill and Carter families have lived here continuously, and today the 800-acre working plantation is operated by the ninth and tenth generations of Hills and Carters. The beautifully well-kept grounds are situated on the banks of the James River. There is a nice gift shop on the premises that carries several items and books for children.

Restored Hampton Carousel with its hand-painted horses. *Courtesy of Hampton Conventions and Tourism.*

Entertainment

If your agenda is left up to the kids, chances are they'll say, "Hang the history. Let's get to the fun!" After all, Tidewater Virginia offers plenty of it, beginning with Busch Gardens and spreading from there to dozens of locations. This section offers some help in choosing among the many options.

Fortunately, even the area's most commercial attractions hold plenty of educational surprises. Just when it seems that all your 8-year-old cares about are monster rides, you find that your "wild thing" wants to spend an hour watching a glass artist working his craft with a blow torch.

Many special programs, theatre performances, and concerts are available for children on weekends and during the summer months. Check the entertainment section of newspapers and local magazines (see page 8) to stay current on dates and times of upcoming events.

Amusement and Theme Parks

Carousel Park

602 Settler's Landing Road, Hampton.

Call the Hampton Visitor Center at 1-800-487-8778 or (757) 727-1101 for additional information. Take I-64 to the Hampton University exit (267). Turn right on Settler's Landing Road and continue over bridge. Proceed 1 block to the Carousel on the left.

- Open April through December: Monday to Saturday, 10:00 a.m. to 8:00 p.m. Sunday, noon to 6:00 p.m.
- Rides are 50 cents.
- Adjacent to Virginia Air and Space Center and *Miss Hampton II* Harbor Cruises.
- Parking across street from Virginia Air and Space Center.

The carousel with its 48 hand-painted horses and two chariots is a rare example of American folk art. It was hand-carved in 1920 and is one of only 200 carousels remaining in the United States. Completely restored to its original condition, the carousel is housed in a new pavilion on the waterfront right next to the Virginia Air and Space Center.

Discovery Zone

Two locations: 1084 W. Mercury Blvd. Hampton (757-825-0035). Follow I-64 to W. Mercury Blvd. (exit 263B). Follow Mercury Blvd. to the second traffic light and turn left into Riverdale Plaza. 401 Oriana Road, Newport News (757-988-3008). Follow I-64 to Jefferson Ave. (exit 255B). Follow Jefferson Ave. to Denbigh Blvd. and turn right on Oriana Road.

- Open daily
- Ages 2-12: $5.99 Monday to Friday, $6.99 weekends. Ages 24 months and under: $3.99 Monday to Friday, $4.99 weekends. Parents play free.
- Socks required to play.
- Birthday parties.
- Identification system for safety.
- Free lockers.

This 20,000-square-foot indoor fun center is designed for fun with physically active children in mind. There is a maze of tunnels to explore and a mountain to climb. Children can zip down a multi-colored rollerslide or conquer a challenging obstacle course. Other activities include a bouncing moon walk and testing skills in the Skill Zone. Relax and have a meal in the DZ Diner.

Shoes are not permitted here, and each child is given a locker to stash shoes and outer garments. Personal safety is an important aspect of the Discovery Zone. Upon entering, each child and accompanying adult receives an identification wrist band bearing identical numbers. Upon exiting the Discovery Zone, the numbers are checked to ascertain that they match.

Williamsburg

Busch Gardens

Route 60 (757-253-3350).

Take I-64 to Route 199 (exit 242A). Continue to Route 60 East and follow signs to Busch Gardens on the right.

- Mid-May through mid-September: daily 10:00 a.m. to 10:00 p.m. and midnight on Saturday. Call for operating schedule during rest of year.
- One-day tickets: adults $28.95, children (3-6) $21.95, under 2 free. Two-day tickets: adults $38.95, children (3-6) $31.95. A three-day combination ticket with Water Country USA is $44.95 and is good for a 14-day period. Group rates are available. All rates are subject to change.

- Parking is $4.00. Free for season pass holders.
- Handicapped accessible. Wheelchairs and strollers available.
- Amusement park rides.
- Restaurants and snack bars.
- Shops.
- Live theatre entertainment.

The park is an action-packed recreation of Old World Europe set on 360 rolling, wooded acres. It is complete with quaint villages, costumed street characters, and foods that are typical of the countries represented. The admission fee entitles visitors to all park activities except food and shopping. Busch Gardens-Williamsburg has been judged the most beautiful theme park in the country for the past 3 years.

Try all three roller coasters including the recently added Drachon Fire which one way or another turns its riders upside down six times. Escape from Pompeii is the park's newest attraction. A quiet boat ride that explores the ancient city soon turns to thrills as Mt. Vesuvius erupts causing a collapsing building, fires, and smoke to "threaten" the occupants of the boat. It's a hot and wet explosive expedition. Enjoy Questor, the fun-filled fantasy ride, or let the children "drive" a Grand Prix racing car over the Le Mans automobile course. When visitors are ready to cool off or rest, there is wonderful live family entertainment that can be enjoyed in air-conditioned comfort. Visit England's Globe Theatre or The Magic Lantern Theatre in the Hastings area. Hunger pangs can be quieted at one of the many restaurants. Experience Germany's Oktoberfest in Das Festhaus and enjoy German food while being entertained by the "oompah" bands and folk dancers. You can have lunch or dinner in Italy while listening to excerpts from an Italian opera. Now may be the time for a relaxing Rhine River Cruise or perhaps a visit to the Roman Rapids, an exciting white-water adventure for the whole family. Prepare to get soaked!

The Globe Theatre hosts the thrilling "4-D" film spectacular, *Haunts of the Old Country*. Follow the "spooky" adventures of 11-year-old Anthony as he meets the ghosts of England's ancient castles. In addition to the 3-D format of the huge screen, viewers of all ages will delight in experiencing cold air, fog, raindrops, and flashes of light for a special "fourth" dimension.

Land of the Dragons will delight the entire family. Friendly, brightly colored dragons fill a fascinating forest. Winding stairways and mysterious towers lead children to a three-story-tall tree house, rides, children's theatre, and interactive play. The youngest visitors will enjoy the animals in the Petting Zoo, and the whole family can relax on the locomotive that chugs its way around the park and the Aeronaut Skyride gondolas which make their way above it all. Grimm's Hollow is an amusement ride area that is just the right size for small visitors. Be sure to take a souvenir photo with one of the resident Clydesdale horses, and a visit to the Feathered Follies Bird Show is always in order.

A young visitor makes the acquaintance of one of the Anheuser-Busch Clydesdales at Busch Gardens, Williamsburg.

Family Funland

801 Merrimac Trail in the James-York Plaza Shopping Mall
(757-220-1400).

Take I-64 to Route 199 West exit (242A). Follow Route 199 to Route 143 West to James-York Plaza on left.

- Open Sunday to Thursday, 11:00 a.m. to 10:00 p.m. Friday and Saturday, 10:00 a.m. to midnight.
- 60 arcade games.
- Nine-hole miniature golf course.
- Birthday party packages.
- Restaurant.

Family Funland offers fun for the entire family. Ride the Krazy-Kars or step into the future while playing Laser Storm, an innovative laser tag game. Young children (and fun-loving parents) will enjoy the soft play unit filled with slides and tunnels. You can play 60 video games or try the nine-hole miniature golf course. Call for information regarding birthday parties.

Williamsburg Amusement Park/Go-Karts Plus

6910 Richmond Road (757-564-7600).

Take I-64 to Lightfoot exit (234A). Turn right at the first traffic light onto Route 60 and continue past the Pottery Factory to the Park on the right.

- Open daily in summer (June, July, August): noon to 11:00 p.m. Spring (April-May) and fall (September-October): Monday to Friday, 5:00 p.m. to 9:00 p.m., weather permitting. Saturday and Sunday, noon to 10:00 p.m.
- Pay per ride. Tickets sell for $1.25 each and rides require one to three tickets. A book of 20 tickets is $20.00. All rates are subject to change.
- Free parking.
- Snack bar.
- Handicapped accessible.

This relatively small park offers attractions for children of all ages. The figure-eight go-kart track is very nice. Drivers must be 58 inches tall. Smaller children may ride in a double car with an adult for one extra ticket. A slicktrack, bumper boats, and basketball shoot-out are also available. In addition, there is an 18-hole miniature golf course. The arcade contains video games, skee ball, and an air-cannon shooting gallery.

Young children will enjoy the battery-powered Kiddie Cars, the Space Train, and Roller Scooters. The Play-port is for children aged 2 to 12.

The snack bar offers hot dogs, ice cream, and soft drinks.

Water Country USA
Route 199 (757-229-9300).

Take I-64 to Route 199 East exit (242B). Follow Route 199 to Park on right.

- Open mid-May through mid-September: 10:00 a.m. to 8:00 p.m. Operating schedule is subject to change.
- One-day tickets: adults $19.95, children (3-6) $15.95. Children under 2 are free. Spectator tickets (non-swimmers): $11.95 plus refundable deposit. There is a three-day combination ticket with Busch Gardens for $44.95. Season passes and special group rates are available. All rates are subject to change.
- Rain check policy.
- Parking is $3.00.
- Restaurants and snack bars.
- Children under 8 must be accompanied by an adult.
- Gift shops.
- Handicapped accessible.

Located on over 40 acres of natural landscaping, the park features over 30 water rides and pool areas. The admission price includes unlimited use of all rides and attractions, the use of shower/bathhouse facilities, lounge chairs, and sun decks. There is free use of life vests for non-swimmers while in the park.

The water rides include Runaway Rapids, which simulates a white water rafting experience; The Amazon, a two-person ride through waterfalls and tunnels; and the Jet Stream, one of the longest water flume rides in the nation. The park's newest attraction is Big Daddy Falls. Almost five stories high, the tube ride takes you down slippery slopes through a 60-foot tunnel, white water rapids, pools, and several water surprises. The Malibu Pipeline is a not-to-be-missed, two-person, mostly enclosed tube ride enhanced by "strobe" lighting and surprise twists and turns. It ends by plunging through a waterfall into a splash pool. Surfer's Bay is an Olympic-sized wave pool. Four-foot waves are produced for 15 minutes, followed by 15 minutes of calm.

Kids Kingdom is a special area for young children. Popular rides include a slippery slide down a seal's back and a plunge down a giant frog's tongue. Cow-A-Bunga is another area for young children and features more slippery slides, waterfalls, fountains, and water cannons. Fun for the whole family is the quiet float ride through scenic woods on the Rambling River.

Live entertainment features the United States High Diving Team performing daily in the Aqua Theatre. The "Sea to Believe" magic show and the "W.C. Duck Water Safety Show," an audience participation show which teaches about water safety, are presented daily in the Lilypad Landing Theatre.

Water Country USA's mascot "W.C. Duck" gives a friendly wave to visitors as they enjoy a leisurely float down the "Ramblin River" at Water Country USA, Williamsburg.

Harbor Cruises

Hampton

Hampton Harbor Cruise

710 Settlers Landing Road (757-727-1102 or 1-800-244-1040).

Take I-64 to Hampton University exit (267). Turn right on Settlers Landing Road and continue over bridge to the Hampton Visitor Center on the left.

- Operates May through September. Two cruises daily in summer: 10:00 a.m. and 2:00 p.m. May and September: cruise at 10:00 a.m. only.
- Adults $13.50, children (6-12) $7.00, under 5 free, seniors $11.00. Group rates available. All rates are subject to change.
- Parking available dockside in garage.
- Cruise past Fort Monroe and Norfolk Naval Base.
- Guided tour of Fort Wool.

The 3-hour cruise of Hampton Roads Harbor is a delightful way to enjoy a summer day. The harbor is remembered in history as the site where the famous clash of the ironclads, the *Monitor* and the *Merrimac*, took place. The fascinating story of the capture of Blackbeard the Pirate, as told by the commentator, captures the imagination of the on-board "sailors." The tour continues along the coast of Old Point Comfort, the site of the present-day Fort Monroe, the only moat-enclosed, active-duty military installation in the United States (see page 31 for additional information).

Strategically located across the mouth of Hampton Roads Harbor is Fort Wool. The pre-Civil War fort was visited by three United States Presidents and was used to guard the entrance of the harbor during the Civil War and World Wars I and II. One of its functions was to serve as an anchor point for a submarine net stretching to Fort Monroe during World War I. Visitors disembark the *Miss Hampton II* and are met by a park ranger who conducts a walking tour of this unique fort. Fort Wool is a superb vantage point to view cargo ships, tankers, and warships from all over the world. (The cruise captain determines whether water conditions permit docking safely. If not, the cruise portion is extended.)

After the tour of Fort Wool, the *Miss Hampton II* cruises the 2-mile waterfront of the Norfolk Naval Base, the largest naval installation in the world, while the narrator provides information regarding each ship that is passed.

Think about making this a full-day adventure by combining the cruise with a visit to the adjacent Carousel Park or the Virginia Air and Space Museum.

Newport News
Harbor Cruise at Wharton's Wharf
530 12th Street (757-245-1533).

Take I-64 to Route 664. Take Route 664 to Terminal Ave. (exit 7) and follow signs to the Harbor Cruise.

- Cruises run April through June at noon. Summer cruises are at noon and 2:00 p.m.
- Adults $12.50, children (under 12) $6.25. Under 3 free.
- Free parking.
- Cruise Newport News Shipyard and Norfolk Naval Base.
- Handicapped accessible.
- Gift shop.
- Restaurant.
- Snack bar on board.

The 2-hour cruise of Hampton Roads harbor, the world's largest harbor, is available every day. While cruising the James River, the boat passes the 550-acre Newport News Shipyard and the narrator comments on the docked ships from around the world that have come to the shipyard for repairs. Many types of ships, such as large nuclear submarines and aircraft carriers, are built, repaired, and fueled here. The boat then crosses the bay to the Norfolk Naval Base, home to 130 different types of naval ships,

Civil War reenactment at Fort Wool, Hampton. *Courtesy of Hampton Conventions and Tourism.*

such as guided missile cruisers, submarines, aircraft carriers, destroyers, and cargo ships, as well as 140 aircraft. The commentator explains the different types of ships and how they are used.

Rest rooms and a snack bar are on board. The adjacent Captain's Galley restaurant features good seafood at reasonable prices.

Music

Hampton

Buckroe Beach

(757-764-2931).

Take I-64 to Mercury Blvd. exit (263B). Follow Mercury Blvd. (Route 258) to left on Pembroke Ave. Continue on Pembroke Ave. (Route 351) to the end.

Enjoy the "Big Band Sound" and dancing on Thursday evenings in August at 7:00 p.m. Bring chairs or blankets. Free.

Fort Monroe

(757-727-3207).

Take I-64 to Mercury Blvd. exit (263B). Follow Mercury Blvd. (Route 258) north about 3 3/4 miles to Fort Monroe.

Delight in the picturesque setting along the river while listening to "Music Under the Stars" by the Continental Army Band performing in free concerts at 7:30 p.m. on Thursday evenings, June through August. Bring chairs or blankets.

Mill Point Park

(757-727-6429).

Take I-64 to the Hampton University exit (267). Turn right on Settlers Landing Road and continue over bridge. Continue 1 block to the park on the right.

Music for listening and dancing takes place in the park on Friday evenings in the summer from 5:00 p.m. to 9:00 p.m. Sandwiches, soft drinks, and ice cream are available. Bring chairs or blankets. Free.

Williamsburg

Summer Breeze Concert Series

Merchants Square on Duke of Gloucester Street (757-229-5676).

During the summer months, bring lawn chairs and blankets and enjoy the free concerts. Concerts begin at 6:00 p.m. and last about

1 1/2 hours. Bring along sandwiches or snacks or perhaps plan on having dinner at one of the close-by restaurants.

Old Dominion Opry

3012 Richmond Road (757-564-0200 or 1-800-2VA-OPRY).

Take I-64 to the Lightfoot exit (234A). Turn left at the first traffic light (Route 60) and follow Route 60 approximately 3 miles to the theatre on the right.

- Open daily except Sunday.
- Show time is 8:00 p.m.
- Adults $14.95, children (under 12) $7.00. Call for information regarding 3:00 p.m. matinees. All rates are subject to change.
- All seats are reserved.
- Free parking.
- Handicapped accessible.

Popular as a delightful family entertainment, Old Dominion Opry features country music and wholesome comedy suitable for children. The cast consists of professional musicians and singers who provide a lively evening of hand-clapping, foot-stomping country music. Popcorn and soft drinks are available for purchase.

Williamsburg Lodge

South England Street in the Historic Area (757-229-1000).

The United States Air Force Band offers free concerts on Wednesday evenings at 7:30 p.m. during July and August. Performances are free but tickets are required. Pick up tickets at the Lodge Bicycle Shop on Saturday at 9:00 a.m. for the following Wednesday concert.

Williamsburg Symphonia

Phi Beta Kappa Memorial Hall, Jamestown Road (757-229-9857).

The Symphonia offers two yearly concerts specifically designed to introduce children to classical music. The fall concert is aimed toward children in the fourth grade and older, while the spring concert is intended for children of preschool age to third grade. Each concert is specially planned to be age-appropriate. Many schools attend the concerts, but seating is also available for families. Tickets for families are $2.00 per person and performances are held on a school day at 10:00 a.m., 11:15 a.m., and 12:45 p.m. Call for dates of concerts and reservations.

Theatre

Colonial Williamsburg

Williamsburg Lodge Auditorium, South England Street, Williamsburg (757-229-1000).

Eighteenth-century plays are performed in costume by professional actors. Admission is charged.

Story Book Theatre

Willett Hall. Willett Drive, off Route 17, Portsmouth (1-800-488-6761).

Four children's theatre productions are produced each year from September through May. Recent performances have included *The Emperor's New Clothes* and *Thumbelina.* Performances take place on Saturdays at 11:00 a.m. Tickets are $5.00 for adults and $3.50 for children. Season tickets for all five productions are $20.00 for adults and $14.00 for children. Call for schedule and ticket information.

Newport News Library

110 Main Street (757-591-4858).

Story Times, a 6-week story session, is designed for children 2 1/2 to 5 years old. In addition, many special events are offered throughout the year. Call for times and dates.

Williamsburg Library Theatre

Williamsburg Regional Library, 515 Scotland Street (757-229-7326).

Live performances by storytellers, musicians, and jugglers, as well as puppet shows, theatre, and family movies are scheduled throughout the year, but especially during the summer months. Call for schedule and ticket information.

Ticket Outlets

Ticketmaster: 1-800-736-2000.

Newport News and Hampton: Tracks Records and Tapes.

Williamsburg: Band Box Records

Spectator Sports

Hampton Roads Admirals

Norfolk Scope, 201 Brambleton Ave., Norfolk (757-640-1212).

The Admirals are a professional ice hockey team and are affiliated with the East Coast Hockey League. The regular season extends from October to March and the playoff season runs through April. All tickets are $6.00 and $7.00. Rates are subject to change.

Peninsula Poseidons

Todd Stadium, 12465 Warwick Blvd., Newport News.

Located on the grounds of the Newport News Administration Building (757-873-1113). The Poseidons are a semi-professional football team of the Mason-Dixon Football League. Call for schedule and ticket information. Tickets may be purchased at the Patrick Henry Mall information booth.

Tidewater Tides

Harbor Park, 150 Park Avenue at the Elizabeth River, Norfolk (757-622-2222).

The Tides are a triple-A baseball team and are the top farm team for the New York Mets. Box seats are $7.00 and reserved seats are $5.50. Parking is $2.00. Rates are subject to change. Call for game schedule.

Fairs and Festivals

January

Laser Light Show

Virginia Living Museum, Newport News (757-595-1900).

Spectacular laser color display set to popular music in the planetarium. Admission is charged.

February

Mardi Gras

Waterside Festival Marketplace, Norfolk (757-627-3300).

March
Military Through the Ages
Jamestown Settlement, Jamestown (757-229-1607).

Reenactment of military tactics and soldiers' camp life from the Middle Ages to modern times.

St. Patrick's Day Parade
Ocean View area of Norfolk (757-587-3548).

April
Annual Children's Easter Eggstravaganza
Town Point Park, Norfolk (757-441-2345).

All-day giant Easter egg hunt and Easter crafts. Special appearance by the Easter Bunny and other stage performances.

Busch Gardens Girl Scout Fest
Busch Gardens, Williamsburg (757-253-3350).

Workshops for the fulfillment of badge requirements. Registration is required. Admission is charged.

Earth Day
Virginia Living Museum, Newport News (757-595-1900).

Learn how to help Mother Earth with her work through activities, environmental exhibits, games, and animal shows. Admission is charged.

Easter Eggs-travaganza
Newport News (757-229-8191).

Arts and crafts, Easter crafts, and handmade items.

Easter Parade of Crafts
Newport News (757-229-8191).

Exhibit and sale of handmade items and Easter crafts.

May
American Heritage Festival
Yorktown Victory Center, Yorktown (757-887-1776).

Crafts demonstrations and interpretations of early American lifestyles. Included in museum admission.

Boy Scout Fest

Water Country USA, Williamsburg
(1-800-343-SWIM).

Workshops for fulfillment of badge requirements. Advance registration required.

Country Festival

Bluebird Gap Farm, Hampton (757-727-6739).

Family festival celebrating the nation's rural heritage. Children learn about farm life. Festivities include sheep shearing, hay rides, horseshoes, crafts, games, and animals.

Jamestown Landing Day

Jamestown Settlement, Jamestown (757-253-4138).

Militia presentations and sailing demonstrations commemorate the anniversary of America's first permanent English settlement in the New World.

Ocean View Beach Festival

Norfolk (757-583-0000).

Norfolk celebrates its waterfront heritage with a parade, carnival rides, exhibits, games, arts and crafts, and fireworks.

June

African American Festival

Mill Point Park, Hampton (757-838-4721).

A family-oriented festival featuring ethnic foods and African and African-American arts and crafts. Enjoy reggae, gospel, and jazz music.

Children's Festival of Friends

Newport News Park, 13560 Jefferson Ave., Newport News
(757-247-8451).

A celebration for children with exhibits by local museums and three stages of performers. $3.00 parking fee.

Harborfest

Norfolk (757-627-5329).

One of the biggest waterfront festivals on the East Coast. Live entertainment, all sorts of gastronomical treats, sailing ships, water shows, air shows, and spectacular fireworks.

Seawall Festival

Portside Festival Area, Portsmouth (757-393-9933).

Family festival with emphasis on activities for children.

Virginia Indian Heritage Festival

Jamestown Settlement, Jamestown (757-253-4138).

Native Americans celebrate their culture with dance, storytelling, demonstrations, crafts, and food. Included in museum admission.

July

Annual Fourth of July Great American Music and Food Festival

Downtown waterfront, Norfolk (757-627-7809).

Concerts, picnic pavilion with hot dogs and crab cakes, children's games and activities, and fireworks.

Blackbeard Pirate Jamboree

Town Point Park, Norfolk (757-441-2345).

Plunder, pillage, and party with Blackbeard. Enjoy children's activities, music, food, and a "dastardly good time for families."

Children's Colonial Days Fair

Yorktown (757-887-1776).

Children are invited to play traditional games, compete in contests, and make crafts to take home. Admission is charged.

Fourth of July Ice Cream Social and Fireworks

Colonial Williamsburg (757-229-1000).

Cake, ice cream, and music on the lawn in front of the Wren Building of the College of William and Mary. After the Social, carry your blankets or folding chairs down Duke of Gloucester Street to enjoy the fireworks provided by Colonial Williamsburg.

Independence Day

Colonial National Historic Park, Yorktown (757-898-3400 ext. 58).

Parade, fife and drum performances, 5K run, arts and crafts, food booths, concerts, and fireworks.

Pine, Pork, and Peanut Festival

Chippokes Plantation State Park, Surry (757-294-3625).

Arts and crafts, food booths, and music.

August

First Assembly Day

Jamestown Settlement, Jamestown (757-898-3400 ext. 58).

The anniversary of the beginnings of representative government in the New World is marked with a commemorative General Assembly session and lively debates by costumed actors.

September

Hampton Bay Days

Downtown Old Hampton (757-727-6122).

Celebrate the Chesapeake Bay with entertainment, seafood, arts and crafts, children's games and entertainment, carnival, waterfront activities, and fireworks.

Hellenic Festival

60 Traverse Road, at Route 17, Newport News (757-874-6958).

Greek arts and crafts, jewelry, imported Greek clothing, Greek music and dance, and food specialties and pastries. There are also pony rides, face painting, petting zoo, and video games.

Jamestown Children's Festival

Jamestown Settlement, Jamestown (757-229-1607).

Festival of seventeenth century fun for children includes Old English games, puppet shows, magic, juggling, Indian arts and crafts, and militia drills. Children must be accompanied by an adult during the festival. Admission is charged.

Publick Times

Colonial Williamsburg (757-229-1000).

A recreation celebrating life in eighteenth century Williamsburg when the general court was in session in the colonial capitol. There are militia reviews, a marketplace selling eighteenth century goods, colonial-style horse racing, military encampments, a mock public hanging, music, storytelling, children's games, and theatre.

State Fair of Virginia

Virginia State Fairgrounds, Richmond (757-228-3200).

A huge fair featuring midway rides, top name entertainment, agricultural competitions, music hall, livestock exhibits, shows, and nightly fireworks. Admission is charged.

Williamsburg Scottish Festival

Williamsburg Winery, 2638 Lake Powell Road, Williamsburg (757-220-0274).

Highland games and festivities with competitions in Highland dancing, athletics, piping, drumming, and fiddling. Also featured is the gathering of clans, music, and food. Admission is charged.

October

An Occasion for the Arts

Merchants Square, Colonial Williamsburg (757-253-0321).

A multi-media festival that features artists and craftsmen, dance, theatre, choral groups, bands, and craft demonstrations.

Annual Children's Fantasy Festival

Town Point Park, Norfolk (757-441-2345).

Magical family fun program featuring children on parade, costumed characters, popular children's musical performers, giant puppets, magic, and mime.

Fall Festival

Newport News Park, Newport News (757-247-8451).

Traditional crafts and trades, folk music, children's corner, and multi-ethnic food pavilion. Parking fee.

Halloween Spooktacular for Kids

Mill Point Park, Hampton (757-727-6429).

Ghoulish entertainment, trick-or-treats, crafts, games, and fun activities.

Oktoberfest

Town Point Park, Norfolk (757-441-2345).

German Festhaus under a big-top tent features German "oom-pah" music, dancing, singing, German foods, and Der Kinder Market for children.

Olde Town Ghost Walk

Portsmouth (757-399-5487).

Professional actors portray "ghosts" inhabiting haunted houses during a walking tour of the Olde Town Historic District. Hot mulled cider is served from the witches' cauldron. Admission is charged.

Yorktown Day Weekend

Yorktown (757-887-1776).

Washington's victory at Yorktown on October 19, 1781 is remembered with military and domestic demonstrations and educational programs.

November

Celebration in Lights

Newport News Park, Newport News (757-247-8451).

Spectacular drive-through event featuring seasonal displays made of thousands of lights.

Foods and Feasts in Seventeenth-Century Virginia

Jamestown Settlement, Jamestown (757-229-1607).

Special-occasion recipes enjoyed by the Jamestown colonists and the Powhatan Indians are prepared. Demonstrations of seventeenth-century food preservation and cooking techniques.

Holidays in the City/Elizabeth River Boat Parade

Town Point Park, Norfolk (757-441-2345).

Lighted boats of all descriptions parade down the Elizabeth River, accompanied by fireworks.

Virginia Thanksgiving Festival

Berkeley Plantation, Charles City County (757-272-3226).

An all-day family festival that commemorates the first Thanksgiving by a reenactment of the landing at Berkeley Hundred. There is also an Indian village, dancers, militia encampments, actors, musicians, arts and crafts, and band concerts. Admission is charged.

December

A Jamestown Christmas

Jamestown Settlement, Jamestown (757-229-1607).

Represents traditional English Christmas celebrations with decorations, performances of period music, and craft demonstrations. A film is shown which compares seventeenth-century English holiday traditions to Christmas at Jamestown. Admission is charged.

Annual Tree Lighting
Yorktown Victory Center, Yorktown (757-887-1776).

The illumination of a large evergreen tree, music, storytelling, and a visit from Santa Claus help celebrate the holiday season.

Christmas at the Mariners' Museum
Newport News (757-595-0368).

The life and Christmas traditions of the nineteenth-century sailor are shown through costumed characters, crafts, and song. Admission is charged.

Christmas Special
Old Dominion Opry, Williamsburg (757-564-0200).

Traditional Christmas in historic Williamsburg is celebrated with hot cider, cookies, music, humor, and a visit from Santa Claus. Admission is charged.

Grand Illumination
Colonial Williamsburg (757-220-7645).

Simultaneous lighting of candles in the windows of the historic buildings on Duke of Gloucester Street, along with music, yule logs, flaming cressets, storytelling, singing, fife and drum parade, and fireworks.

Hampton Holly Days
Downtown Hampton at the Waterfront (757-727-1102).

Holiday parade and Illuminated Parade of Sail. Breakfast with Santa.

Holiday Crafts Workshop
Yorktown Victory Center, Yorktown (757-887-1776).

Families make seasonal decorations and crafts. Admission is charged.

Spirit of Hampton Roads Holly Days Parade
Downtown Hampton (757-727-1102).

Illuminated nighttime street parade with marching bands, floats, equestrian units, and the arrival of Santa and Mrs. Claus.

Williamsburg Christmas Parade
Duke of Gloucester Street and Richmond Road.

Marching bands, floats, and Santa Claus as the holiday season is ushered into the Historic Area. The parade begins on Duke of Gloucester Street and continues up Richmond Road.

Parks, Nature, and Beaches

Urban planners say that counting the number and variety of parks is one sure way to determine the quality of life in just about any area. If that's true, Tidewater Virginia ranks high on the funmeter because it offers so many places for picnicking, swimming, boating, exploring nature, and just "hanging out."

Best of all, the parks are open daily and have free admission unless noted otherwise. The Nature Centers found in several of the parks are fountains of information. Talks and exhibits at the centers explain wildlife, river inhabitants, and park history. Please remember, the Virginia Living Museum (see page 36) is an outstanding nature experience not to be missed.

Take advantage of the unusual special attractions available at several of the parks. Check out the 2-hour, guided canoe trips at York River State Park which provide the opportunity to dip and glide through the area's salt marshes for reasonably close encounters with a variety of waterfowl and wildlife.

For a more domesticated experience, try Bluebird Gap Farm. Old Macdonald would be hard pressed to match the variety of farm animals available for petting and observing. An oink-oink here, a cluck-cluck there, will particularly impress the smallest family members.

The option of choosing a Chesapeake Bay beach or a visit to a beach on the York or James Rivers is for you to decide.

Hampton Parks

Briarfield Park

Corner of Briarfield Road and Big Bethel Road.

For information call the Hampton Parks Department at 757-727-6347. Take I-64 to the Mercury Blvd. exit (263A). Follow Mercury Blvd. (Route 258) to Jefferson Ave. (Route 143). Turn left on Jefferson Ave., then left on Briarfield Road to the park entrance on the right.

- Open year-round.
- Tennis courts.
- Softball fields.

- Playground.
- Restrooms.

Briarfield Park is a delightful family park. Wonderful for picnics, the park contains four picnic shelters that can be reserved. There are five lighted tennis courts as well as four lighted softball fields and a nice children's playground.

Gosnold's Hope Park

1901 Little Back River Road (757-850-5116).

Take I-64 to Mercury Blvd. exit (263B). Follow Mercury Blvd. (Route 258) approximately 2 miles to King Street. Turn left on King Street and right on Little Back River Road to park entrance on the left.

- Open daily 7:00 a.m. to sunset.
- Picnic shelters.
- Playground.
- Bicycle motorcross track.
- Boat ramp.
- Fitness trail.
- Campsites.
- Restroom facilities.
- Bridle trails.

Hampton's largest developed city park, Gosnold's Hope Park has much to offer. Complete with picnic shelters that may be reserved, it is another delightful spot for a family outing. There is a nice children's playground, a fitness trail, and a boat ramp. The unusual feature of this park is the bicycle motorcross track. Sanctioned by the National Bicycle League, races are held the first and third Sundays of each month. Registration takes place noon to 1:30 p.m. on the day of the race.

Hampton Neighborhood Parks

James M. Mason Memorial Park

Adjacent to Darling Stadium on Victoria Blvd.

This quiet community park is open year-round. There is a playground, gazebo, park benches, picnic tables and grills, and a small jogging trail.

Mill Point Park

Downtown at the corner of Queen and Eaton Streets.

Located on the waterfront, the park offers a picturesque view of the Hampton River. A 300-seat amphitheater and stage area is the home for the free summer concerts sponsored by Hampton Frolics and the Hampton Recreation Department. The Bay Days Festival (see page 65) is held here. Admission to the park and concerts is free.

Ridgway Park

Mercury Blvd. just north of Fox Hill Road.

This small neighborhood park contains a picnic shelter, children's playground, and a lake.

Newport News Parks

Deer Park

Jefferson Ave. and J. Clyde Morris Blvd. (757-591-4848).

Take I-64 to J. Clyde Morris Blvd. exit (258A). Follow J. Clyde Morris Blvd. (Route 17) to Jefferson Ave. (Route 143). Left on Jefferson Ave. to the park entrance on the right.

Located very close to the Virginia Living Museum (see page 36), Deer Park is a lovely, natural extension to a visit to the VLM. The park contains playing fields, hiking and jogging trails, and picnicking facilities. In addition, there are floral gardens, freshwater fishing, and playground equipment. Interesting interpretive programs are also offered. Call for program information.

Harwood Mill Reservoir Park

Oriana Road (York County), Newport News (757-886-7911).

Take I-64 to J. Clyde Morris Blvd. exit (258B). Follow J. Clyde Morris Blvd. (Route 17) north, which becomes George Washington Memorial Highway. Continue on Route 17 to Oriana Road. Turn left on Oriana Road to the park entrance on the left.

- Open daily, sunrise to sunset.
- Picnic facilities.
- Boat ramp and boat rentals.
- Freshwater fishing.
- Hiking and jogging trails.
- Bicycle trails.
- Playground equipment.
- Snack bar.

A heavily wooded park bordering the reservoir, Harwood Mill Reservoir Park is a lovely spot to enjoy a summer afternoon. Boat rentals are available during the season. Boaters wishing to use the ramp for private boats must obtain a permit before launching. No gasoline or diesel engines are permitted. Fishermen must possess a valid Virginia fishing license.

Huntington Park
Warwick Blvd. at the James River Bridge.

For information call the Newport News Park Headquarters at 757-886-7911. Take I-64 to Mercury Blvd. exit (263A). Continue south on Mercury Blvd. (Route 258) to Warwick Blvd. (Route 60). Turn right on Warwick Blvd. to the park entrance on the left. The park is adjacent to the War Memorial Museum and the YMCA.

- Open daily until 10:00 p.m.
- Fort Fun.
- Picnic tables and shelters.
- Beach.
- Playgrounds.
- Tennis.
- Rental boats and boat ramp.
- Snack bar.
- Gardens.
- Playing fields.

Located on the grounds of the War Memorial Museum (see page 38), this city park with its lovely floral gardens overlooks the James River and contains a sandy beach area. Fishermen may purchase blood worms, peelers, and ice. The snack bar sells sandwiches, hot dogs, soft drinks, and snacks.

Fort Fun, a large wooden playground area, contains a ship with a crow's nest, a "haunted" castle, mazes, tunnels, bridges, and a children's fishing pier.

For additional recreation, there are playing fields and tennis courts. Call (757) 247-8587 for information regarding tennis lessons, clinics, and camps. A call to that number will also reserve a court. Plan to picnic in the park after a visit to the War Memorial Museum or before or after a class or activity at the nearby YMCA (see page 85).

Newport News Park

Jefferson Ave. and Fort Eustis Blvd. (757-886-7911).

Take I-64 to Ft. Eustis Blvd. exit (250B). Turn left on Jefferson Ave. (Route 143) to the park entrance on the right.

- Open daily, sunrise to sunset.
- Two 18-hole public golf courses. Call (757) 886-2848 to reserve tee time.
- Picnic tables and shelters.
- Boating.
- Hiking trails.
- Bridle trails.
- Bicycle trails. Rental bicycles available.
- Camping.
- Interpretive Center.

Newport News Park's 8000 acres make it the largest municipal park east of the Mississippi River, and it is actually larger than any Virginia state park. Nearly 450 white tail deer make their home here.

In addition to recreation facilities, this park features Deer Run Golf Course with two 18-hole championship courses, two putting greens, a driving range, snack bar, and pro shop. Golf lessons are available for children and adults. The park has one of the largest and most thorough junior golf programs in the state. Call (757) 886-2848 for information.

The bridle trails are another unusual feature of the park. Horse lovers may trailer in their own horses and ride the trails.

Stop by the Interpretive Center for information regarding the park's natural and historical resources. This huge park also plays host to many special events throughout the year. For a listing of the fairs and festivals that take place in the park, please turn to pages 63, 66, and 67.

Newport News Neighborhood Parks

There are several small neighborhood parks located in Newport News that offer a variety of recreational facilities. Check them out if you find yourself in the neighborhood. For additional information call Newport News Park Headquarters at 757-886-7911.

Anderson Park/Peterson's Yacht Basin

6th St. and Oak Ave.

This park contains playing fields, basketball courts, a beach, biking trails, boat ramp, saltwater fishing, interpretive programs, picnic facilities, playground equipment, and tennis courts.

Beachlake Park

Longmeadow Drive.

Basketball courts, freshwater fishing, and hiking/jogging trails are located here.

Christopher Newport Park

26th St. and West Ave.

Floral gardens and historical features are located in this pretty park. There is a good view of the James River and the Newport News shipyard.

Denbigh Park and Boat Ramp

Located at the end of Denbigh Blvd.

Boat rentals, saltwater fishing, and hiking/jogging trails are available. The public boat ramps are open 5:00 a.m. to 9:00 p.m. daily.

Highland Court Park

Highland Ave.

Playground equipment and tennis courts are available.

King-Lincoln Park

South end of Jefferson Ave.

This park contains basketball courts, beach, saltwater fishing, a nature center, picnicking facilities, playground equipment, rest rooms, tennis courts, and an entertainment stage.

Williamsburg Parks

Kidsburg

3793 Ironbound Road in the Mid-County Park.

A large and wonderful playground, Kidsburg is a study in community cooperation. Local businesses donated the funds and the construction of the imaginative wooden structures was supplied by volunteers. A park-naming contest was held in the local schools and the name Kidsburg was selected as winner.

All sorts of wonderful apparatus encourage physical activity and imaginative play. There is a Tarzan swing, a music wall, a theatre, and a fort complete with bridges, tunnels, and slides. There is also a covered glider swing, two 10-tire bouncers, a covered wagon with two wooden horses, a tire ladder, and a wonderful cable bridge.

The tot lot for the youngest set contains swings, a monkey swing beam, a look-out deck, a fort with ladders and slides, and "King George's coach."

Adults can join the kids on the equipment or watch the fun from one of the benches. Picnic tables and restrooms are available.

Waller Mill Park

West of Williamsburg on Airport Road (Route 645) between Route 60 and I-64 (757-220-6178).

- Open daily, March to mid-December, sunrise to sunset.
- Picnic tables and shelters.
- Hiking trails.
- Playing fields.
- Playground.
- Nature trails.
- Row boats, canoes, and pedal boats.
- Fishing.
- Seniors Walking Course.
- Nature Trail for the blind.

This pretty, 2300-acre Williamsburg city park is situated around the reservoir. The 343-acre lake is open for fishing, boating, canoeing, and pedal boating, and has a tunnel connecting the upper and lower portions of the lake. Nestled among the trees bordering the lake are numerous picnic tables, three shelters, and wooden playground equipment.

There are three nice hiking trails for picturesque walks around the reservoir. The Bayberry Nature Trail is 1 1/2 miles long. The longer Lookout Tower Trail is 3 1/2 miles and passes a lookout tower from which there is a great view of the reservoir. The Dogwood Trail is 3 1/4 miles in length and has a par course with 12 exercise stations. There is also a Seniors Walking Course with 14 stretching exercise stations.

The lake is home to many noisy ducks and geese who are extremely tame and are always looking for food. They are a delight for all, especially small children. A small food machine is available for those who wish to feed these birds (and everyone does).

Visitors with a Virginia fishing license may fish from the pier with no charge, or from a fishing boat ($4.00 per day), or from their own boat ($3.00 per day). Please note that gasoline and diesel motors are not permitted.

Row boats and canoes are available for rent for $3.00 per hour and pedal boats rent for $2.00 per half hour.

York River State Park
5526 Riverview Road, Croaker, Williamsburg (757-566-3036).

Take I-64 to Croaker exit (231B). Go north on State Route 607 for 1 mile. Turn right on Route 600 to the park entrance.

- Open daily, 8:00 a.m. to dusk.
- Honor system parking. Memorial Day to Labor Day: $1.50 per car on weekends, $1.00 on weekdays. Wednesdays are free. March and April, September and October: $1.00 on weekends, free on weekdays. Parking is free during the remainder of the year.
- Picnic areas, hiking trails, bicycle trails, picnic shelters, bridle trails, and boat ramp.
- Interpretive programs are available March to October. There are a few programs scheduled during the winter months. Call (757) 564-9057 for information.
- Canoe trips.
- Fishing.
- Visitor Center.
- Junior Ranger workshops.
- Environmental education.
- Handicapped accessible.

The beautiful 2502-acre park is known for its rare and delicate estuarine environment. Fresh and salt water meet to create a habitat rich in marine and plant life. Activities in the Visitor Center focus on the history, use, and preservation of the York River and its marshes. The Center is open Thursday through Sunday from Memorial Day to Labor Day and is open weekends during the remainder of the year.

To help make your visit to the park a grand adventure for the children, do try to take advantage of the unique activities offered to visitors. Brochures available in the Visitor Center describe the wide variety of unusual activities scheduled. For example, guided canoe trips are offered April to October and focus on life in the salt marshes. The trips last about 2 hours, and children between the ages of 3 and 15 must be accompanied by a parent or guardian. Children under 3 are not permitted on the trips. Fees are $4.00 per person and $3.00 per person for groups of four or more. Reservations are required. Trips are scheduled for Saturdays, 8:30 a.m. to 10:30 a.m. and Sundays, 4:00 p.m. to 6:00 p.m. (Bring along insect repellent, sun screen, hat, and beverage.)

On the beach are activities where participants may seine, cast, and dip nets. Aquatic animals caught in the nets must be released. Other activities include bird watching and beachcombing.

The hiking trails meander through woodlands, saltwater marshes, and pine and hardwood forests. Try one of the unusual hiking trips offered, such as the history hike or perhaps one of the night hikes.

Environmental education facilities available in the park include a wetlab and an amphitheater. A variety of equipment for the study of the park inhabitants is available for school and other groups. Call the park for further information.

The fishing regulations require a valid Virginia fishing license. There is a bass creel limit of five per day with a 12-inch minimum.

Other recreational possibilities include volleyball and horseshoes. Equipment can be checked out at the Visitor Center. The Visitor Center has a small book and gift shop.

The Junior Ranger Program, offered for children aged 7 to 12, is designed to teach responsible conservation practices, natural science, and the duties of a park ranger. "Hands-on" activities are a part of the program.

Williamsburg Neighborhood Parks

Mid-County District Park

3793 Ironbound Road.

The centrally located park is home to Kidsburg. (See separate listing for Kidsburg on page 74.) It also contains playing fields with scoreboard and bleachers, three tennis courts, basketball courts, playground, picnic table, shelters and grills, rest room facilities, and a fitness trail.

Quarterpath Park

202 Quarterpath Road (757-220-6170).

Located close by the Colonial Williamsburg Historic Area. From the intersection of Francis and York Streets, follow York Street (Route 60 east) a half mile to Quarterpath Road on the right. The entrance to the park is almost immediately on the right.

- Open daily, 8:00 a.m. to 10:00 p.m.
- Lighted tennis courts.
- Lighted playing fields.
- Outdoor basketball courts.
- Outdoor swimming pool.
- Gymnasium.
- Playground.
- Indoor fitness/walking course.

Operated by the Williamsburg Department of Recreation, the park offers a variety of recreational programs and classes. The three outdoor lighted tennis courts are open in summer until 10:00 p.m. There are three lighted outdoor ball fields and two outdoor basketball courts. To help alleviate the heat of hot summer days, take a swim in the outdoor, Z-shaped pool and let the little ones splash about in the large baby pool. The playground contains both regular and baby swings, a climbing ladder, and other equipment.

There are all kinds of programs and classes running the gamut from judo to swimming to cheerleading clinics. For a detailed description of the programs and classes offered, see Quarterpath Park on page 93, which refers to sports in the area.

An extension to the park is off Ironbound Road across the street from the Virginia Gazette building. Located here are seven additional lighted tennis courts.

Children's Farms and Petting Zoos

Bluebird Gap Farm

Pine Chapel Road, Hampton (757-727-6739).

Take I-64 to Mercury Blvd. exit (263B). Turn right on Coliseum Drive. Turn right again on Pine Chapel Road. Continue just over the hill to the entrance gates of the farm on the left.

- Open Wednesday to Saturday, 9:00 a.m. to 5:00 p.m. Closed Monday, Tuesday, and holidays. Closed on Wednesday when major holidays fall on Mondays or Tuesdays.
- Free admission.
- Free parking.
- Handicapped accessible.
- Playground.
- Picnic area.
- Nature trail.
- Concessions.

Bluebird Gap Farm is a wonderful outing for children, especially the very young. This small farm houses a variety of farm animals ranging from chickens, ducks, turkeys, and rabbits to larger animals, such as horses, cows, goats, sheep, and pigs. Many of these animals may be petted, and children may also purchase animal feed from a machine for 25 cents. Also on exhibit are other animals native to Virginia, such as deer, mountain lions, and bobcats.

Children can learn about a variety of growing plants as there is a vegetable and flower garden, and each plant is identified by a marker. A very nice playground is on the premises and just outside the farm is a park with a picnic area.

SPCA Petting Zoo and Exotic Area
523 J. Clyde Morris Blvd. Newport News (757-595-1399).

Take I-64 to J. Clyde Morris Blvd. exit (258A) about 2 miles to SPCA on right. The SPCA is located across from the Virginia Living Museum.

- Open daily, Monday to Friday 10:00 a.m. to 5:00 p.m.; Saturday, 10:00 a.m. to 4:30 p.m. Sunday noon to 5:00 p.m. Closed holidays and may be closed during rainy weather.
- Admission is $1.00 per person. Children aged 2 and under are free.
- Handicapped accessible.
- Gift shop.

The wide variety of domestic and exotic animals will delight children of all ages. Youngsters can wander about with goats, sheep, chickens, several llamas, ducks, and geese. There are also pigs, donkeys, and a turtle. Feed machines are available, and for 25 cents children can help feed the animals. In addition, some interesting exotic animals are enclosed in zoo cages. On exhibit are

Siberian tigers, African mandrills, leopards, jaguars, a gray fox, kangaroos, a Canada lynx, and an otter.

The Woof and Purr Gift Shop is staffed by volunteers and monies raised are for all the animals living in the Petting Zoo and Exotic Animals Area as well as for all the animals living at the shelter.

Local Beaches

Beach lovers will enjoy the Chesapeake Bay and river beaches located on the Peninsula. Ocean aficionados may enjoy a day trip to world-famous Virginia Beach. For information regarding Virginia Beach, see page 108.

Buckroe Beach and Park

Located at the end of Buckroe Ave., Hampton (757-727-6197).

Take I-64 to Mercury Blvd. exit (263B). Follow Mercury Blvd. (Route 258) to left on Pembroke Ave. Continue on Pembroke Ave. (Route 351) to the end.

- Open Memorial Day to Labor Day.
- Free admission.
- Free 3-hour parking.
- Lifeguards on duty.
- Fishing pier.
- Concessions.
- Picnic shelters.
- Restrooms.

Located on beautiful Chesapeake Bay, Buckroe Beach is very popular with families. There is a very nice sandy beach, perfect for kids of all ages to construct imaginative sand creations. Lifeguards are on duty during the official season. Picnic tables and concessions are available, and there is a fishing pier. Buckroe Park, which is adjacent to the beach, is home to summer concerts, film festivals, and art festivals. Try it!

Grandview Nature Preserve and Beach

Located off Beach Road, Hampton.

Take I-64 to Mercury Blvd. exit (263B). Follow Mercury Blvd. (Route 258) to left on Pembroke Ave. (Route 351) to left on Old Buckroe Road. Turn right on Beach Road and follow it to the end.

Families interested in wildlife, ecological studies, and water bird observations will especially enjoy Grandview Nature Preserve. But almost everyone will enjoy walking and hiking along the Preserve's sandy beaches. The park consists of 578 acres of marshlands that includes a beach that stretches for 2 1/2 miles.

Huntington Beach

Warwick Blvd. at James River Bridge.

Take I-64 to Mercury Blvd. exit (263A). Continue south on Mercury Blvd. (Route 258) and cross Warwick Blvd. (Route 60). Turn right at entrance to beach.

- Open Memorial Day to Labor Day.
- Free admission.
- Free parking.
- Lifeguard on duty.
- Concession.
- Restrooms.
- Picnic shelters.

Located on the James River, this sandy beach is a perfect place to spend a warm summer day. A concession stand and restrooms are available on the beach. The beach is adjacent to Huntington Park, which contains picnic tables and shelters. Also located in the park is Fort Fun, a wonderful play area for kids to unwind. For further information call Newport News Park Headquarters at (757) 886-7911.

York Beach

Water Street, Yorktown.

Take I-64 to Yorktown exit (247B). Follow the signs to the Colonial Parkway to Yorktown.

- Open Memorial Day to Labor Day.
- Sand beach.
- Lifeguard.
- Restrooms.
- Roped-off swimming area.

This nice, small, sandy beach is located on the York River. There is a lifeguard on duty during the season. Alcoholic beverages, pets, and loud music are prohibited. Picnic facilities are located at the south end of the beach.

Sports

There are times when families yearn for the peace that can be found in an afternoon of fishing from the pier at Buckroe Beach, or in the fresh air of a horseback ride at Newport News Park.

Then again, there are times when families want to mix it up amid the noise and excitement at a youth league soccer or basketball game. Whatever your frame of mind, you can find ideas for the right outlet in this chapter. The sports are listed by locality to facilitate locating nearby athletic opportunities. Have fun!

Hampton

Hampton Recreation Department
(757) 727-6197.

A call to this number will provide information regarding neighborhood soccer, football, basketball, track and field, wrestling, and girls' softball.

Hampton YMCA
1320 LaSalle Ave. (757) 722-9044.

The YMCA offers a full gymnasium with free weights and Cybex fitness equipment. An indoor cushion track is featured as well as racquetball and basketball facilities. There are also many youth sports programs and classes. In addition, child care for preschoolers and before- and after-school daycare is available.

Community Centers
The Community Centers house gymnasiums and game rooms. Activities are available for children aged 6 and up. Free play in the game rooms emphasizes tabletop games such as table tennis, pool, and soccer. The gyms contain basketball hoops and volleyball nets and are open for free play, but there are no league teams. The Old Hampton Community Center features a swimming pool. Call (757) 727-1124 for aquatic information.

North Hampton Community Center
1435 Todds Lane (757) 825-4805.

North Phoebus Community Center
249 West Chamberlin Ave. (757) 727-1160.

Old Hampton Community Center
201 Lincoln Street (757) 727-6197.

Bicycling
Bicycle Motorcross Track
901 Little Back River Road (757) 850-5116.

Sanctioned by the National Bicycle League, the motorcross track is located in Gosnold's Hope Park. Races are held on the first and third Sundays of each month. Registration takes place noon to 1:30 p.m. on the day of the race. Call for additional information.

Bowling
Century Lanes Bowling Center
519 E. Pembroke Ave. (757) 722-2551.

Sparetimes Bowling Center
1907 N. Armistead Ave. (757) 838-2121.

Fishing Piers
Buckroe Beach Fishing Pier
330 S. Resort Blvd. (757) 851-9146.

Grandview Fishing Pier
54 S. Bonita Drive (757) 851-2811.

Golf
The Hamptons
320 Butler Farm Road (757) 766-9148.

This new public golf course offers a junior golf program for children. Group lessons for the various age groups are given during the summer months. The program is coordinated with the Parks and Recreation Department. Private lessons are also available.

Woodlands Golf Course

9 Woodland Road (757) 727-1195.

Youngsters may play on this public course, but lessons for children are not available.

Public Boat Ramps

Sunset Boat Ramp

Ivy Home Road.

Gosnold's Hope Park

901 Little Back River Road (757) 850-5116.

Skateboarding

Skateboard Park

9 Woodland Road, adjacent to the tennis courts and golf course (757) 727-1195.

Swimming Pools

Old Hampton Community Center

201 Lincoln Street (757) 727-1123.

Tennis

Call the Hampton Parks Department for additional information (757) 727-6347.

Briarfield Park

Corner of Briarfield and Big Bethel Roads.

The park contains five lighted courts.

Hampton Tennis Center

9 Woodland Road (757) 727-1194.

The Center contains seven soft-clay courts with a two-court stadium and is one of the few public facilities in the Mid-Atlantic area that has soft-clay courts. There is also a fully stocked pro shop, a lounge area, restrooms, and ample parking. There are no membership dues or yearly fees. Court time is $5.00 per hour. Both private and group classes are held and a ball machine may be rented.

Tennis clinics are available for children aged 4 through 18. There is also a tennis camp for children aged 10 through 18. Instruction is provided by six local pros. Each session is 4 hours long. Beginner and intermediate camp sessions are scheduled for mornings and camp sessions for advanced players are held in the afternoon. Call the Center for information regarding schedules and fees.

The Hamptons

320 Butler Farm Road (757) 766-9148.

Track and Field

Hershey's Track and Field

This annual event held in May is for boys and girls aged 9 to 14 and is held at Darling Stadium. Call (757) 727-6197 for further information.

National Age Group Track and Field

Boys and girls aged 9 to 14 come from all parts of the country to participate in this annual 5-day meet held in July at Darling Stadium. Call (757) 727-6197 for information.

Newport News

Call the Newport News Park Headquarters at (757) 886-7911 or the Park Department Youth Activities Services at (757) 591-4892 for additional information.

The Peninsula YMCA

7827 Warwick Blvd. (757) 245-0047.

The YMCA is a microcosm of a world of sports. Offered are a full gymnasium, aerobics room, nautilus and free weights, five racquetball courts, and a heated, indoor swimming pool. Lessons are available for swimming, lifeguarding, scuba, water safety, fitness, soccer, basketball, T-ball, volleyball, karate, racquetball, and tumbling. The classes are open to children of all age levels, including preschoolers aged 3 to 5, and toddlers aged 1 to 3. There is a day care center for children aged 2 to 5 where lunch is served. Call for information and rates.

The indoor soccer leagues are for children aged 6 to 12. Each child plays a minimum of one half of each game. Boys and girls aged 6 to 12 are also eligible to play in the outdoor soccer leagues as well as the basketball leagues. Some children in this age group might like to try the youth karate.

Younger children aged 6 to 8 may be interested in playing T-ball. Other possibilities include gymnastics for beginners and inter-mediates as well as for children with advanced skills. Preschool sports for 3- to 5-year-olds include kinder T-ball, kinder soccer, kinder basketball, and "tumbleweeds," a tumbling program. The aquatic program is designed for 1- to 3-year-olds, 3- to 5-year-olds, and older children aged 6 to 15.

Archery

Newport News Park Archery Range has been issued a five-star rating by the National Field Archers Association (NFAA). The range consists of a practice range (seven shooting lanes) and three target ranges (28 lanes per range). All archers must first complete the Archery Range Safety Course which teaches general safety rules as well as rules specific to this range. Reservations are required and children must be accompanied by a certified adult. Call (757) 886-7912 for additional information.

Biking

Newport News Park, Jefferson Ave. and Fort Eustis Blvd. (757) 886-7912, contains a 5.3-mile bikeway for bicyclists, walkers, and runners. Bicyclists may ride their own bikes or rent one for $3.00 per hour.

Boating

Newport News Park, Lee Hall Fishing Area, and Harwood's Mill Reservoir are idyllic spots for this sport. Oars, paddles, and per-sonal flotation devices are provided. Canoes rent for $3.00 per hour and paddleboats are $4.00 per hour. No one under 16 years of age may rent watercraft.

Bowling

Denbigh Lanes

Sherwood Shopping Center (757) 877-9966.

Fair Lanes

12407 Warwick Blvd., Hidenwood (757) 595-2221.

Newmarket Bowling

630 79th Street, Newmarket Shopping Center (757) 245-2818.

Fishing

Saltwater fishing piers are located at Hilton School, King-Lincoln Park, and Denbigh Park. Freshwater fishing is available at Lee Hall and Harwood's Mill Reservoir.

Golf

Deer Run Golf Course

Ft. Eustis Blvd. (757) 886-7925.

Greens fees for students to play 18 holes are $5.75, plus tax. Keep in mind that rates are subject to change. Both group and individual instruction is offered.

Gymnastics

Gym Sports

700 Thimble Shoals Blvd., Suite 102 (757) 873-2198.

Gym Sports offers gymnastic classes for boys and girls. The programs for preschoolers are 45 minutes. The classes for school-age children, elementary through high school, are 1 hour in length. Competitive gymnastic teams are another possibility for interested boys and girls. Gymnastic classes are also offered for moms and tots ranging in age from 18 months to 3 years. A summer day camp which operates from 9:00 a.m. to 2:00 p.m. features gymnastics, arts and crafts, and water activities. Call for information and fees.

Horseback Riding

Newport News Park

Horse owners can enjoy a trot over the bridle trails.

Yorke Stables

1052 George Emerson Lane, Tabb (757) 591-8791.

Riding and lessons for children aged 6 years and up.

Miniature Golf

Putt-Putt Golf

Warwick Village Shopping Center, Warwick Blvd., Hilton (757) 596-7562.

Open daily. Hours vary seasonally. Three well-kept courses are available for play. A snack bar on the premises offers chips, candy, hot dogs, and ice cream. Many children enjoy mini-golf birthday parties, and birthday celebrants can enjoy seeing their name in lights. Prizes are awarded.

Neighborhood Sports Leagues

The Newport News Parks and Recreation Department sponsors many neighborhood leagues in a variety of sports. Below is a listing of the sports available as well as the telephone numbers needed to obtain additional information.

Baseball/Softball

Boys and girls aged 6 to 18 can register by bringing a parent and birth certificate to registration. The leagues are divided by residential boundaries within the city. Fast-pitch softball leagues are also available for girls aged 9 to 15.

Basketball

Boys and girls 6 to 15 may participate. There is no fee but a parent and birth certificate are required at time of registration. Call (757) 591-4892 for information.

Cheerleading

Boys and girls aged 6 to 14 can cheer for youth football games and take part in local cheerleading competitions. Instructional classes include gymnastics and tumbling for cheerleaders. Call (757) 247-8451.

Field Hockey

Boys and girls aged 9 to 18 are eligible to participate. All games are held at the Menchville High Field Hockey Field. Call (757) 247-8451.

Soccer

There are several age-grouped soccer leagues available for boys and girls aged 5 to 15. Call (757) 591-4892.

Programs for Handicapped Children

Therapeutic Recreation Center

325 Main St. (757) 591-4889.

The therapeutic after-school program is designed for individuals with mental and/or physical disabilities. The variety of activities available include swimming, special olympic skills practice, and field trips.

Boy Scout Troop 217 is for boys with disabilities. Youngsters interested in learning about scouting, wildlife, camping, cooking out, and providing community service are invited to participate. Call (757) 591-4889 for information.

Camp Discovery is a summer day camp for physically and mentally disabled children. Camp Cheers is a summer day camp for emotionally disturbed children and children with behavior problems. Activities at both camps include field trips, swimming, and boating. To obtain an information packet regarding either of these programs call (757) 591-4889.

Roller Skating
Peninsula Family Skating Center
307 Main St. (757) 599-4769.

The Center is the only indoor skating rink in Newport News. Skaters may either rent skates or bring their own. Your child may enjoy having a skating birthday party here. Call to make arrangements.

Skateboarding
Newport News Deer Park Municipal Center
11523 Jefferson Ave. (757) 591-4847.

Open daily, the Center features two metal ramps plus a large concrete practice area. Approved knee and elbow pads, helmet, and parental consent are required. Call for fee information.

Sports Centers
The following centers are host to a number of sport activities that include volleyball, basketball, whiffle ball, indoor soccer, wrestling, cheerleading, and board games.

Jenkins
(757) 881-5411.

Richneck
(757) 886-7952.

Magruder
(757) 247-8504.

Saunders
(757) 591-4842.

Newsome Park
(757) 247-8435.

Warwick Recreation
(757) 591-4892.

Swimming Pools

Doris Miller Pool
2814 Wickham Ave. (757) 247-1401.

Magruder Swimming Pool
1712 Chestnut Ave. (757) 247-5934.

The Peninsula YMCA
7848 Warwick Blvd. (757) 245-0047.

Tennis

Huntington Park Tennis Center
Warwick Blvd. at James River Bridge (757) 247-8587.

Clinics and camps for all levels feature instruction, video analysis, stroke review, and supervised match play. Call for court reservations and fee information.

Anderson Park
16th Street and Oak Ave.

Highland Court Park
Highland Ave.

King-Lincoln Park
South end of Jefferson Ave.

Centre Court Racquet Club
12445 Warwick Blvd. (757) 595-5639.

Children aged 4 to 18 may participate in group tennis lessons which are offered daily except Sundays. Instructional levels are available for beginners who have never played before up through ranked tournament players.

Williamsburg

Williamsburg Department of Recreation

202 Quarterpath Road (757) 220-6170.

A wide range of sports and activities are available for residents of Williamsburg, James City County, and York County. Offered are tennis lessons and youth tennis leagues for ages 8 to 12. Swimming lessons in the outdoor pool are divided into two-week sessions and run Monday through Thursday. Basketball games and clinics are offered for kindergartners through twelfth graders. Gymnastics are available for 3- to 5-year-olds and 6- to 12-year-olds. Karate is available for ages 4 to 6 and 7 to 18. Youth bowling is offered for ages 6 to 18. Other sport possibilities include softball for kindergartners through twelfth graders as well as volleyball for children aged 9 to 18. Dance programs are available for ages 3 and up and feature jazz, tap, and ballet. Call for fee schedule.

Williamsburg/James City County Recreation Center

5301 Longhill Road (757) 220-4700.

Residents of either the city of Williamsburg or James City County may join the Recreation Center. There is a daily admission fee for non-member residents as well as for non-residents. Facilities include an outstanding 12-lane, 25-meter indoor pool. There are also locker rooms, saunas, two racquetball courts which can be converted to basketball or volleyball courts, Cybex fitness equipment, exercise equipment, and snack bar. The pool is open Monday to Thursday, 6:00 a.m. to 9:00 p.m. and until 8:00 p.m. on Friday. Saturday it is open from 9:00 a.m. to 6:00 p.m. and Sunday, 1:00 p.m. to 6:00 p.m. Three lanes are open for lap swimming at all times. Swimming lessons are available for every age group and skill level.

There are also many classes and activities for children. Preschoolers aged 3 to 6 may enroll in kid's chef, tumble tots, gym swim, tot tennis, and half-pint soccer. Children between the ages of 6 and 12 can try youth karate, gymnastics, or dance with volleyball or basketball. The Center also sponsors a before- and after-school program which is a structured recreation offering homework time, games, sports, arts and crafts, local field trips, parties, and outdoor play.

Bicycle Rentals
Bikes Unlimited
759 Scotland Street (757) 229-4620.

Bikesmith
15 York Street (757) 229-9858.

Colonial Williamsburg Lodge
South England Street (757) 229-1000.

Boating
Waller Mill Park
West of Williamsburg on Airport Road (757) 220-6178.

Rowboats, canoes, and pedal boats are available for rent.

York River State Park
5526 Riverview Road, Croaker (757) 566-3036.

The park sponsors wonderful canoe trips (see page 76 for further information).

Bowling
Williamsburg Bowl
5544 Olde Towne Road (757) 565-3311.

Horesback Riding
Carlton Farms
3516 Mott Lane (757) 220-3553 or 220-3576.

Lessons are available for boys and girls 5 years and up. Call to arrange for an assessment lesson to determine your child's skill level and proper placement.

Cedar Valley Farm
804-A Lightfoot Road (757) 565-2585.

One-hour lessons are offered to children 6 years and up.

Miniature Golf

Go Karts Plus

6910 Richmond Road, next to the Williamsburg Pottery
(757) 564-7600.

Open daily. Summer (June, July, August): 11:00 a.m. to 11:00 p.m.
Spring and fall (April-May, September-October): Monday to
Friday, 5:00 p.m. to 9:00 p.m. Saturday, open noon to 10:00 p.m.;
Sunday, noon to 9:00 p.m.

Mini-Golf of America

1901 Richmond Road, next to Morrison's Cafeteria
(757) 229-7200.

Open daily. Summer (June, July, August): 1:00 p.m. to late evening.
Spring and fall (April-May, September-October): Monday-Friday,
5:00 p.m. to late evening. Saturday and Sunday, 1:00 p.m. to late
evening.

Swimming

Indigo Park Pool

154 Stanley Drive (757) 229-8473.

The small outdoor, neighborhood pool has many amenities to
offer. Membership is open to families, couples, and singles.
Family potluck dinners are held twice during the summer.
Swimming lessons are available for all ages and skill levels. The
Indigo Park Stingrays, a competitive swim team, is for swimmers
18 years of age and younger. Meets are held weekly and there are
daily practices.

Quarterpath Park Pool

202 Quarterpath Road (757) 220-6170.

See the listing under Williamsburg Department of Recreation for
additional information.

Williamsburg Community Pool

1228 Richmond Road (757) 229-7791.

This outdoor pool offers free Red Cross swimming lessons for
members. Children aged 6 to 18 are invited to join the competitive
swim team. The pool is open daily during the summer months.

Williamsburg/James City County Recreation Center

5301 Longhill Road (757) 220-4700.

Pool patrons must be 11 or older for unaccompanied swimming. Children 10 and under must have adult supervision. (See the Williamsburg/James City County listing on page 91 for additional information.)

Tennis

The following three locations are municipal courts. Play is free during daylight hours and $2.00 per hour when courts are lighted. For reservations call (757) 220-6176.

Kiwanis Municipal Park

Off Ironbound Road,
across from the Virginia Gazette Building
(757) 220-6176.

There are seven lighted courts.

Mid-County District Park

3793 Ironbound Road (757) 229-1232.

Three courts are available.

Quarterpath Park

202 Quarterpath Road.

There are three unlit courts.

Track and Field

Hershey Track Meet

Boys and girls between the ages of 9 and 14 are eligible to compete. Birth certificates must be presented during registration which takes place in early May at the Williamsburg/James City County Recreation Center or at the Williamsburg Recreation Center. The local meet is held at the College of William and Mary. Children who place either first or second may compete in the Eastern District Meet held in Hampton. Winners continue on to the State Meet held in Charlottesville.

Day Trips

Sometimes, when the stress of modern family life mounts to a misery rating, the best answer is to steal a day from a hectic schedule and slip away for a short trip to a special place.

The Tidewater area was made for such escapes. Hopewell, Norfolk, Portsmouth, Surry, and Virginia Beach are all within an hour's driving time. Just in case you're looking for a few ideas, we created the following section as a guide. Remember, have fun and keep the pace light.

Hopewell

School-age children and adults with an interest in history will enjoy a visit to this city. The Hopewell Visitor Center, located at 201D Randolph Square, is the best place to obtain brochures, maps, and directions to the various sites. The Broadway Cafeteria, located at the corner of City Point Road and Route 10, and the Captain's Cove restaurant, located on the waterfront, are good lunch options.

Appomattox Manor

Stop at the Hopewell Visitor Center for map and directions.
(757) 541-2206.

- Open daily 8:30 a.m. to 4:30 p.m.
- Free admission.
- Special summer program for children.

Appomattox Manor is located at the confluence of the James and Appomattox Rivers. The site was shelled by the British during the American Revolutionary War, and during the time of the Civil War this area was one of the world's busiest seaports. The 23-room manor was patented in 1635 by Captain Francis Eppes, who arrived in Hopewell from England in that year. It was owned by the descendants of the Eppes family for the next 340 years, until 1979, when the property was taken over by the National Park Service.

The manor displays the Eppes' original Victorian furnishings which were removed to a safe place during the Union occupation and later returned. Appomattox Manor was General Grant's Headquarters in 1864-65 during the siege of Petersburg and Richmond, and from here Grant directed the attack upon Lee's forces. Visitors can enter and inspect the original two-room "Headquarters Cabin" of General Grant that is on display on its original site. It is interesting to note that President Lincoln spent 3 weeks in nearby City Point in 1865. The beautiful grounds surrounding the manor are well-kept and overlook the two rivers. Outbuildings consist of a dairy and a smoke house.

Weston Manor

Located near the Hopewell Yacht Club off 21st Ave. on the historic Appomattox River. Call (757) 458-4682 or the Hopewell Visitor Center (757) 541-2206.

- Open April through October: Monday to Friday, 10:00 a.m. to 4:00 p.m. Limited hours on weekends. Call first.
- Adults $5.00, children under 12 are free if parents have tickets. Colonial Heritage Trail block tickets are available for $17.00 and include Weston Manor, Bacon's Castle, Smith's Fort Plantation, Brandon Plantation Gardens, and Chippokes State Park. All rates are subject to change.
- Outdoor concerts in summer.

Owned by the same family, probably longer than any land in the United States, Weston Manor, built about 1735, is one of the few plantation homes remaining on the lower Appomattox River. It represents a chronicle of the lives of the three generations of Eppes family members who lived here. A plan of the property shows it to be part of the royal land granted to Francis Eppes in 1635.

The home contains original eighteenth-century furniture and some reproductions. The floors and windowpanes are original. A typically colonial feature of the house is the oversized "funeral door," built to accommodate the carrying of a coffin to and from the house.

During the Civil War, a cannonball was shot through the dining room window and penetrated the ceiling of the house. During the restoration of the manor, the cannonball was dislodged and fell through the ceiling and is now exhibited for visitors.

In the latter part of the war, the home was occupied by General Sheridan and other officers. Look for their names scratched into a glass windowpane. The house was also used as a temporary hospital for federal troops during the occupation by General Ulysses S. Grant.

Outdoor concerts are held during the summer on the patio behind the house. Call for dates and times.

Norfolk

A city noted for its naval history, Norfolk offers families a multitude of exciting things to see and do. While visiting, be sure to save time for lunch at Doumar's on the corner of 20th Street and Monticello Avenue. Have an old-fashioned ice cream soda, hot dog, or hamburger. Perhaps a homemade ice cream cone is more to your liking. Doumar's introduced the world's first ice cream cone at the St. Louis Exposition in 1904.

The Chrysler Museum

242 West Olney Road (757-664-6200).

Take I-64 to Route 264 to the Brambleton Ave. exit. Follow the signs to the Chrysler Museum.

- Open Tuesday to Saturday, 10:00 a.m. to 4:00 p.m., and Sunday, 1:00 p.m. to 5:00 p.m. Closed Monday.
- Admission by suggested donation.
- Family Fun programs.
- Historic Houses Outreach Program.
- Restaurant.
- Gift shop.

The Museum contains one of the premier art collections in the country, and exhibits span the centuries from 2700 B.C. to the present. It contains an internationally famous glass collection and also has the only museum gallery in Virginia devoted solely to photography. Although art museums in general are usually not favored by children, the Chrysler Museum offers several tours devoted to children and their families. Every other Sunday the Museum hosts free Family Fun programs which may include puppet shows, dance and music concerts, and mime. There is also a wide variety of gallery activities and "hands-on" workshops for the entire family. During the summer months, there is an Art Camp for ages 6 to 12. For further information regarding children's tours, workshops, and classes, contact the Family Fun program at (757) 622-1211.

Visitors can enjoy lunch at "Palettes," the Museum's café, which offers a special children's menu.

Shake Hands with History is a part of the Historic Houses program for children. This program presents aspects of the history of the United States in an entertaining format for the entire family. The Museum's Department of Historic Houses also offers extensive educational programs geared for kindergarten through twelfth-grade school groups. The programs focus on the seventeenth- and eighteenth-century lifestyles of Virginians. Programs are offered at the Adam Thoroughgood House, the Willoughby-Baylor House, and the Moses Meyer House. For more information call (757) 664-6283.

Nauticus, The National Maritime Center

One Waterside Drive (757-664-1000 or 800-664-1080).

Take I-64 to Route 264 West and exit on Waterside Drive. Follow the signs to the museum. Parking is available at the Norfolk City Garage located across the street.

- Open daily in summer, 10:00 a.m. to 7:00 p.m. Remainder of year open Tuesday through Sunday, 10:00 a.m. to 5:00 p.m. Closed Thanksgiving, Christmas, and New Year's Day.
- Adults $7.50, students (13-17) $6.50, children (6-12) $5.00. Children under 5 are free. Nauticus Theater Virtual Adventures and Aegis Theatre are $2.50 each for adults and students and $1.50 each for children. The all-inclusive Explorer package is $14.00 for adults, $13.00 for students, and $8.50 for children. All rates are subject to change.
- Interactive exhibits.
- Theaters.
- Virtual reality.
- Aquarium.
- Hampton Roads Naval Museum
- Nauticus International Pier.
- Café.
- Gift shop.

Nauticus has been called "the museum of the future." It is part science center, part interactive museum, and part aquarium.

Begin the tour by boarding the world's longest inclined people mover which takes visitors to the main exhibit area on the third floor. Many exciting adventures await you. Land your plane on an aircraft carrier or pilot your ocean-going vessel through the wind, fog, and reefs of busy San Francisco Bay Harbor. Sit in the captain's chair, observe the harbor from the bridge, and play real-life "warship" by operating sonar devices. Watch the Navy's Blue Angels in action and hold video "conversations" with Navy personnel. Learn how weather information is gathered and be a weatherman on the Nauticus weather channel. Pet the creatures of the sea in the tidal touchpool. You can even pet a shark! Be sure to see "The Living Sea" shown in the Nauticus Theater. The film takes audiences on a journey of discovery about the world's oceans and their countless bizarre yet beautiful creatures.

Take a simulated underwater thrill ride in a "virtual reality" submarine. Your research pod will take you on a journey complete with prehistoric monsters and bounty hunters while you search for the Loch Ness Monster. Visitors can also take part in an action-packed multi-media battle simulation on a Navy Aegis missile destroyer.

Tape your own TV weather forecast at the Nauticus Weather Channel. *Courtesy of Nauticus, The National Maritime Center.*

The Hampton Roads Naval Museum, operated by the U.S. Navy, presents a chronological history of the Navy in this region, including the American Revolution, the Civil War, and the two World Wars. The Naval Museum is free and open to the public.

Take a lunch break at Ray's Café and visit the unique gift shop. Be sure to stroll out on the pier and see the visiting ships docked there. For information on ship public visitation, call (757) 441-2345. On some summer evenings, spectacular laser light shows with music and fireworks brighten the sky over the pier.

The Virginia Zoo
3500 Granby Street (757-441-5227).

Take I-64 through the Hampton Roads Tunnel to the Granby Street exit. Stay on Granby and follow the signs to the Zoo on the left.

- Open daily (except Christmas and New Year's Day), 10:00 a.m. to 5:00 p.m.
- Adults $2.00, children (2-11) $1.00, senior citizens $1.00. There is a free hour on Sunday and Monday, 4:00 p.m. to 5:00 p.m. Rates are subject to change.
- Summer Safari programs for children.
- Virginia Farmland exhibit.
- Picnic facilities in Lafayette Park.
- Safari Shop.
- Concession stand.
- Handicapped accessible.
- Educational tours available.

Zoo animals—from the rare, white rhinoceros to the white-handed gibbon, to the East African crowned crane, to the red-necked wallaby—are exhibited in a lovely, landscaped park setting. Of special interest is the new state-of-the-art tiger exhibit. The daily elephant demonstrations are enjoyed by visitors of all ages.

Also noteworthy are the unusual and fascinating programs and classes offered to children and families. For example, try the Zoo Snooze. Children aged 6 and older, along with a parent or grandparent, can spend a night in the zoo. Participants bring their own supper or purchase a box supper from the zoo's "Beastro" and spend the evening visiting behind the scenes, playing games, and taking a night walk through the zoo. After an early breakfast, participants see how animals start the day, deliver animal breakfasts, and meet some of the keepers. Zoo Tots is designed for 3- to 5-year-olds with a parent or grandparent. Children may meet some baby animals, feed some fuzzy friends, and enjoy crafts and games. There are many other classes available. Call (757) 627-8003 for information and rates.

Another exciting possibility is the Summer Safari. This summer day camp's objective is to learn by doing. Certified teachers take campers behind the scenes to touch, feed, and observe zoo animals through tours and live animal demonstrations. The camp is for children in first through fifth grade and all participants must have completed kindergarten. There are both half-day and full-day sessions. Families who are members of the Virginia Zoological Society receive a discount on classes and programs. Call (757) 624-9937 for information and fees.

Still another unusual area of the Zoo is the Virginia Farmland exhibit. Visitors can see examples of livestock as well as the typical architecture of a Virginia farm in the early 1800's.

The Beastro concession stand offers a Kids' Feed Bag which consists of a peanut butter and jelly sandwich, cookie, and soft drink packaged in an animal safari food carton. The Safari Shop carries all sorts of intriguing items that will amuse and educate youngsters.

The Waterside
Located on the Norfolk waterfront on Waterside Drive
(757-627-3300).

Take I-64 to Route 264 to Waterside Drive exit and follow the signs to Waterside.

- Marketplace hours: open daily Monday to Saturday, 10:00 a.m. to 9:00 p.m. Sunday, noon to 6:00 p.m.

Fun for the whole family can be found at The Waterside. The upper level contains many types of shops such as fashion apparel, gift shops, book stores, and specialty shops that feature jewelry, hats, shoes, and music. There are several shops that cater to children offering clothing, toys and games, and there is one shop devoted to a huge menagerie of stuffed animals. The lower level is made up of specialty food shops in the food court. Choose from a selection of seafood, hamburgers, ethnic foods, desserts, candy, and ice cream. There is surely something for everyone. Several good restaurants can be found on both levels for those who prefer a more leisurely meal.

Saturday afternoon, between the hours of noon and 6:00 p.m., The Waterside presents a free program of activities and entertainments that are family-oriented. Costumed Disney characters offer free face painting, and visitors can participate in sing-a-longs and arts and crafts.

Town Point Park, located adjacent to The Marketplace, is the site of many festivals and special events such as the annual Harborfest. Many art shows, craft fairs, and musical entertainments also take place here. (See page 61 for a listing of fairs and festivals.)

Several cruises depart from the Waterside dock. Children will especially enjoy a cruise on the Mississippi-style riverboat or the schooner. There is also a harbor cruise dinner ship.

Portsmouth

The old, waterfront city of Portsmouth lies just over the James River Bridge and the new Monitor-Merrimac Tunnel. There is much to see and do here. Try the Portsmouth Trolley Tour for an overview of the city and then visit one or two of the museums suggested below. Stop by Portside during the lunch hour and be entertained by the music and dance programs for children. And guess what—they're free!

The Children's Museum of Virginia

221 High Street (757-393-8393 or 1-800-PORTS-VA).

From the Upper Peninsula, take either the James River Bridge (Route 17 South) or the Monitor-Merrimac Tunnel (Route 664 South) to Route 17 in Churchland, and follow Route 17 to High Street.

- Open daily 10:00 a.m. to 5:00 p.m. Summer: open 9:00 a.m. to 9:00 p.m.
- Admission is $3.00 per person over the age of 2. Museum Key Pass block tickets are available for $5.00 and include the Children's Museum, the Lightship Museum, the Arts Center, the Portsmouth Naval Museum, and the Virginia Sports Hall of Fame.
- "Hands-on" museum.

Youngsters and the young at heart will have an exciting learning experience at this unusual "hands-on" museum filled with over 60 interactive activities. Have you ever seen a bubble? From the inside? If not, put yourself inside the Bubble Dome. Climb the wall at the Rock Climb and learn some basic principles of physics at the Science Circus. Pretend to be someone else and try the "dress-ups" to become an "instant" fireman or doctor. Explore the creative process and the use of light and color in Art Moves, or make music at Aerobic Sound. And of course the computer mind-benders are there to challenge your brain. The New2Do Gallery features popular touring exhibits.

Another favorite standout is the 64-seat planetarium where the seasonally changing shows reflect the changes in the heavenly bodies.

Lightship Museum

Located on the waterfront at the foot of London Blvd. (757-393-8741).

From I-64 take either the James River Bridge (Route 17 South) or the Monitor-Merrimac Tunnel to Route 17 in Churchland. Follow Route 17 to High Street and continue to downtown Portsmouth and the waterfront.

- Open Tuesday to Saturday, 10:00 a.m. to 5:00 p.m., and Sunday, 1:00 p.m. to 5:00 p.m. Closed Monday.
- $1.50 admission. Museum Key Pass block tickets for $5.00 are available and include the Lightship Museum, the Portsmouth Naval Museum, the Children's Museum, the Arts Center, and the Virginia Sports Hall of Fame.

Ships were once equipped with lights on their masts and anchored off the coastline to guide mariners through the waters at night. The floating lightship *Portsmouth* was commissioned in 1915 and has been restored to its original condition. In 1989, it became Portsmouth's second National Historic Landmark. Visitors can board the vessel and see the ship's kitchen, the captain's and crew's quarters, as well as the engine and boiler rooms. Tours for third graders are offered in the spring.

Dressing-up at the Children's Museum, Portsmouth. *Courtesy of The Children's Museum.*

Mike's Trainland and Lancaster Train and Toy Museum

5661 Shoulder Hill Road, Suffolk (757-484-4224).

Take I-64 to Mercury Blvd. South (exit 263A). Continue on Mercury Blvd. over the James River Bridge (Route 17). Follow Route 17 to the Bennett's Creek area and follow the sign to Trainland on the right.

- Open daily 10:00 a.m. to 6:00 p.m. and Sunday, noon to 6:00 p.m.
- Free admission. There is a donation box.
- Free parking.
- Repair and restoration services.
- Gift shop.
- "Hands-on" opportunities.

Children and adults alike will enjoy a leisurely tour through this unusual museum. It contains the Mid-Atlantic's largest indoor Gauge 1 layout. Youngsters will be delighted and fascinated by the variety of layouts that include a railway garden, circus, freight, and passenger train motifs. With a push of a button, children can make the trains whistle, or turn the radar detectors, or light up the water tower. Just deposit 25 cents to make the trains run and hear the hypnotic chugging sound of the locomotives.

There is an interesting display of antique trains, toys, and railroad memorabilia, many of which date back to the early part of the century. Another part of the museum features a huge Playmobile layout with a gigantic selection of Playmobile toys for sale.

The gift shop contains just about everything train hobbyists could possibly desire. Another feature is the Christmas Shop which contains doll houses, miniature general stores, furniture, and accessories.

Outdoors, there is an actual caboose. Climb aboard and pretend to travel to some exotic faraway destination.

Portsmouth Naval Shipyard Museum

Located at Riverfront Park on the Elizabeth River (757-393-8591).

Take I-64 to either the James River Bridge or the Monitor-Merrimac Tunnel (Route 664 South) to Route 17 in Churchland. Follow Route 17 to High Street and continue to downtown Portsmouth and the waterfront.

- Open Tuesday to Saturday, 10:00 a.m. to 5:00 p.m., and Sunday, 1:00 p.m. to 5:00 p.m. Closed Monday.
- Admission is $1.00. Children under 2 are free. Museum Key Pass block tickets are available for $5.00 and include the Shipyard Museum, the Lightship Museum, the Children's Museum, the Arts Center, and the Virginia Sports Hall of Fame.

The Museum was established in 1949 within the nation's oldest shipyard, the Norfolk Naval Shipyard in Portsmouth, and was later moved to its present waterfront location. Exhibited is a chronology of early Portsmouth dating from 1608, when Captain John Smith sailed from Jamestown to explore the Elizabeth River, to 1781, the year Benedict Arnold occupied and fortified Portsmouth.

On exhibit are a variety of model ships from pleasure craft to aircraft carriers. An 1880 Gatling gun, a cannon mount, a helmet of the type worn by navy divers, and Union and Confederate uniforms are just a few of the many items on display.

Virginia Sports Hall of Fame

420 High Street (757-393-8031).

Take I-64 to either the James River Bridge (Route 17 South) or the Monitor-Merrimac Tunnel (Route 664 South) to Route 17 in Churchland, and follow Route 17 to High Street.

- Open Tuesday to Saturday, 10:00 a.m. to 5:00 p.m., and Sunday, 1:00 p.m. to 5:00 p.m. Closed Monday.
- Free admission. Museum Key Pass block tickets are available for $5.00 and include the Sports Hall of Fame, the Naval Shipyard Museum, the Lightship Museum, the Arts Center, and the Children's Museum.
- Handicapped accessible.

Of interest to older children, the purpose of the museum is to honor those who have accomplished exceptional achievement or service to sports in Virginia. Just about every sport is represented, and the records of outstanding teams and individuals are included in this cavalcade of Virginia sports history.

Surry

Enjoy a wonderful 20-minute ferry ride from Jamestown to Surry. Bring along some bread and let the children feed the sea gulls that swoop around the ferry as it makes its way across the James River. A delightful lunch sure to please youngsters (as well as adults) can be had at the Surry House Restaurant in Surry (see page 130 for more information). Or, if picnics are more to your liking, pack a lunch to enjoy alongside the river at Chippokes State Park.

Bacon's Castle

Route 10 (757-357-5976).

Take the ferry from Jamestown to Surry. Follow Route 31 to Route 10 East. Continue on Route 10 for 6 miles to Bacon's Castle on the left.

- Open Tuesday to Saturday, 10:00 a.m. to 4:00 p.m., and Sunday, noon to 4:00 p.m. Closed Monday.
- Adults $5.00, students $1.00. Virginia Colonial Trail block tickets are available for $17.00 and include Bacon's Castle, Weston Manor and Smith's Fort Plantations, Brandon Plantation Gardens, and Chippokes State Park.

Visitors are surprised to learn that the "Castle" is not a castle at all, and that Nathaniel Bacon, the pre-Revolutionary rebel, did not build it, and, in fact, never even lived here. Assuming the leadership of a band of insurgents, Nathaniel Bacon led a rebellion against the rule of the Royal Governor, William Berkeley. His troops occupied the home for 4 months. It is from this occupation by the rebels that Bacon's Castle received its present name.

Built in 1665 by Arthur Allen, it is the oldest and largest documented brick house in English North America. Much of the house still has the original beams and floors. There are two floors to visit as well as the basement, where a portion of the floor is still covered by the original 1665 bricks. While touring the garret, be sure to have the children ask about the ghosts. Two of the interesting items found in one of the bedrooms on the second floor are the rope bed and bed wrench. If asked, the guide will demonstrate how the old saying, "Good night, sleep tight" originated. Outdoors, the formal gardens have been partially restored on the spot where archeological evidence has indicated the original gardens once stood.

Chippokes Plantation State Park

Route 634, Surry (757-294-3625).

Take the ferry from Jamestown to Surry and follow Route 31 to

Route 10 East. Continue on Route 10 East to left on Route 634. Continue approximately 4 miles to Park entrance.

- Open daily year-round.
- Parking fee: weekends, $1.50 per car; weekdays, $1.00.
- Virginia Colonial Trail block tickets are available for $17.00 and include Chippokes State Park, Weston Manor and Smith's Fort Plantations, Bacon's Castle, and Brandon Plantation Gardens. All rates subject to change.
- Handicapped accessible.
- Mansion tours.
- Antique Farm and Forestry Museum. Rates subject to change.
- Olympic-sized outdoor pool and baby pool. Rates subject to change.
- Farm Tour Road.
- Visitor Center
- Hiking and bicycle trails.
- Picnic areas.
- Working farm.
- Formal gardens.

Chippokes Plantation, established in 1619, is the oldest continually farmed property in the United States. Located on the James River, the Visitor Center offers slide shows, historical exhibits of the history of the Plantation and its inhabitants, and descriptions of the early commerce on the river. The various facilities of the Park are open seasonally and there is a nominal fee. Call the Park for information regarding hours and fees.

The Olympic-sized pool is open Memorial Day through Labor Day. Hourly bike rentals are available. Tours of the mansion are conducted during the summer months. The Pork, Peanuts, and Pine Festival is held on the grounds of the Park in July.

Exhibits at the Antique Farm and Forestry Museum represent various stages of farm life, including building a farm, preparing the soil, and planting and harvesting. Additional exhibits feature tools used by tradesmen such as the blacksmith, wheelwright, cooper, and cobbler. One of the oldest rare artifacts on display is an oxen-drawn plow which dates from the early 1600's. Another is a pre-Civil War, wooden-tooth cultivator. Also displayed is an early, hand-held sickle. In later years, farmers used a reaper, and still later the grain binder. By seeing the actual machinery, children learn how each invention affected the farmer and his family. Call (757) 786-7950 for hours and fee.

Virginia Beach Area

For a fun-filled day at the ocean, a visit to Virginia Beach is perfect. Sand, sun, boardwalk, ocean swimming, "munchies," and amusements are sure children pleasers. If this is not enough, try visiting one of the museums or amusement parks described below.

Ocean Breeze Festival Park

700 S. Birdneck Road (757-422-4444 or 422-0718).

Take I-64 to the Virginia Beach/Norfolk Expressway (Route 44 East). Follow Route 44 East to exit 8 and continue to Park on left.

- Open daily, Memorial Day through Labor Day.
- Admission fee.

The delightful Park includes Wildwater Rapids, a 9 1/2-acre water park which features a wave pool, twister slides, speed slides, and children's activity pools. Another section of the Park is called Motorworld. Here visitors find Grand Prix race cars, go-carts, and bumper boats. There is also an exciting and amusing 36-hole miniature golf course. Strike Zone offers the opportunity for would-be major leaguers to try hitting everything from fast balls to slow-pitch softballs.

Virginia Beach

Take I-64 to the Virginia Beach/Norfolk Expressway (Route 44 East) and follow it to the ocean.

Noted for being one of the outstanding beaches on the eastern seaboard, Virginia Beach's 28 miles of shoreline are bounded on one side by the Atlantic Ocean and on the other by the Chesapeake Bay. Lifeguards are on duty from 9:30 a.m. to 6:00 p.m. daily, Memorial Day through Labor Day. There are public restrooms at 17th, 24th, and 30th Streets on the oceanfront. These facilities do not have changing areas, but there is a public bathhouse at 1st Street and Atlantic Avenue which is operated by the Lighthouse restaurant; call (757) 428-7974 for rates on parking, restrooms, showers, dressing areas, and rentals.

There are more than 1,000 on-street metered spaces at the oceanfront. Public lots can be found at 19th and Pacific Avenue and at 4th Street and Atlantic Avenue. Free parking is available on a first-come basis at the Pavilion on 19th Street. Handicapped ramps to the beach are at 2nd, 13th, 14th, 17th, and 20th Streets. Street handicapped parking is at 2nd, 7th, 16th, and 33rd Streets. The Visitor Information Center, 2100 Parks Avenue, is open from 9:00 a.m. to 8:00 p.m. daily during the summer. Call 800-VA BEACH for additional beach information.

The famous boardwalk is an integral part of the beach's attraction. There are restaurants, pedestrian parks, and seasonal entertainment to delight visitors of all ages. Water sports to suit most enthusiasts are available, such as surfing, windsurfing, jet skiing, sailing, and canoeing. Fishermen can fish from piers on the ocean or the bay or from a headboat. Golfers will find 10 public golf courses, and families will enjoy the challenge of several miniature golf courses. Tennis players will find more than 188 public tennis courts.

Restaurants range from fast food to gourmet. Additional restaurants and many shops can be found on Atlantic and Pacific Avenues. Other amusements include the Atlantic Fun Center on 25th Street and Atlantic Avenue which houses arcade games, a fun house, and a dance floor for all ages. Beach Bumper Boats for young children is located at 2109 Pacific Avenue. The Haunted Mansion is on 20th Street and Atlantic Avenue.

Enjoying the surf and sand at Virginia Beach.

Virginia Marine Science Museum
717 General Booth Blvd. (757-437-4949).

Take I-64 to the Virginia Beach/Norfolk Expressway (Route 44 East). Follow Route 44 East to exit 8. Continue on Birdneck Road to General Booth Blvd. to Museum on left.

- Open September through May: Monday to Saturday, 9:00 a.m. to 5:00 p.m. Mid-June through August: Monday to Saturday, 9:00 a.m. to 9:00 p.m., and Sunday, 9:00 a.m. to 5:00 p.m.
- Admission is charged.
- Aquarium.
- "Hands-on" exhibits.
- Outdoor saltwater marsh boardwalk.
- Birthday parties

This outstanding, "hands-on" museum will truly delight visitors of every age group, but children especially will enjoy the unique exhibits. Try making waves or start a storm in the weather room; guide the fiddler crab safely through the prey and predator maze; climb in an Indian dugout; inspect insects through microscopes; touch live sea animals. The fun, excitement, and educational opportunities go on and on. There are no "Do not touch" signs to be found here. Instead, visitors are encouraged to push buttons, move levers, touch sea creatures, and play games. Children will be fascinated by the marine life found in the 50,000-gallon

Visitors can learn about the history of the Chesapeake Bay at the Virginia Marine Science Museum, Virginia Beach. *Courtesy of the Virginia Marine Science Museum.*

aquarium. There is a small amphitheater where visitors can learn more about the inhabitants of the aquarium. There is even a special computer to help youngsters "design" a fish.

Outdoors, a boardwalk meanders around a salt marsh where waterfowl and other marsh animals may be seen. Or take one of the scheduled tours for an in-depth look at the marsh.

To schedule a birthday party, contact the Education Department at (757) 437-4949. The Museum provides invitations, an educational program, and gifts. Parents provide food, beverages, and decorations. The parties are for children aged 3 through 11, and each group is entertained with an age-appropriate program. All programs feature a "hands-on" activity.

Shopping

Shopping with the kids can be quite vexing unless, of course, you're buying something for them. Then your little "wild things" start sporting their halos, hoping they'll score a new toy as a reward. With these trials and tribulations in mind, this section helps you identify the best options. Included are specialty clothing shops, out-of-the-ordinary book stores, and toy and hobby shops that stimulate the imagination and are fun to explore. Be aware that most museum gift shops feature inexpensive items for children that are both unusual and delightful. For example, toys reminiscent of eighteenth-century playthings are to be found in many museum shops.

Several large shopping malls are located throughout the Peninsula. Coliseum Mall and Newmarket Mall are located on Mercury Boulevard in Hampton. Patrick Henry Mall is on Jefferson Avenue in Newport News. Williamsburg is home to The Outlet Mall, Berkeley Commons, and The Williamsburg Pottery Factory, all of which are located on Richmond Road. Most of the major department stores in the malls contain very nice children's departments. Many of the "chain" stores have been omitted here to conserve space.

Hampton

Clothing and Furniture

Kids Mart

1800 W. Mercury Blvd. in Coliseum Mall (757) 825-0827.

Clothing for infants through preteens.

Books

Old Hampton Book Store

555 Settlers Landing Road (757) 722-1454.

A charming store that carries books for children. A special children's reading corner invites browsing.

Toys, Games, Hobbies, and Dolls

Hampton Hobby House

Coliseum Mall (757) 826-3400.

Kits for making models of cars, boats, and airplanes can be found here. There is a wide selection of model paints and art supplies. The store also carries trains and kites. Stamp and coin collectors can find albums and numismatic and philatelic materials here.

Kay Bee Toys

Coliseum Mall (757) 838-3593.

Features toys at a discount.

My Doll Shoppe, Inc.

555 Settlers Landing Road (757) 723-0000.

A delightful store containing dolls of every size and description, doll clothing, and doll houses. In addition, there is a large and wonderful collection of stuffed animals, as well as educational toys and puzzles.

Toys R Us

4019 West Mercury Blvd. (757) 838-4787.

Probably the best known discount toy and children's furniture supermarket store in the United States.

Newport News

Clothing and Furniture

Rainbow Kids

Newmarket Mall (757) 826-0723.

This shop carries infant and toddler clothing, boys' clothing up to size 18, and clothing for girls up to size 16.

Books

Chelsea's Books

121-J Grafton Station Lane, Washington Square Shopping Center, Grafton (757) 898-7208.

A lovely selection of children's books and unusual greeting cards.

The Bookworm

14501-J Warwick Blvd.
(757) 874-7554.

A new and used paperback book store which carries a nice selection of used children's books that sell for half off the list price.

Parent Teacher Supply Co.

5005 Victory Blvd. in the Village Square at Kiln Creek
(757) 877-0500.

This store features teaching aids and supplies for teachers and parents. Books, games, posters, and other teaching tools can be found here.

Toys, Games, Hobbies, and Dolls

Hungate's Arts, Crafts, and Hobbies

Patrick Henry Mall (757) 249-5112.

Headquarters for hobby, craft, and art supplies. There is a large selection of paints and canvasses, doll houses, model cars, trains, boats, and rockets.

Kay Bee Toys

Patrick Henry Mall
(757) 249-3147.

A well-stocked discount toy store.

Teachers' Store

13749-B Warwick Blvd.
(757) 874-8380.

Devoted almost entirely to teacher supplies, the store carries educational books, games, and posters. Look for the intriguingly shaped, blank jigsaw puzzles. Children can draw or color the pumpkin-, egg-, or leaf-shaped puzzles, take them apart, and try to assemble them again.

Toy Works

455 Oriana Road, Newport Crossing Shopping Center (757) 875-0456.

A large toy supermarket that carries all types of toys suitable for infants on up. Large outdoor play equipment, high chairs, and car seats are also to be found here.

Williamsburg

Clothing Stores

Carter's Children's Wear

Berkeley Commons on Richmond Road
(757) 565-3440.

Labels found here include Carter, Tykes, Baby Dior, and Junior Dior. The clothing ranges in size from infant to size 7 for boys and infant to size 6X for girls. Pajamas and underwear are carried up to size 14.

Casey's of Williamsburg

345 Duke of Gloucester Street in Merchants Square
(757) 229-2311.

Features traditional and designer clothing for children.

The Carousel

Duke of Gloucester Street in Merchants Square (757) 229-1710.

This delightful store carries a complete line of beautiful clothing and accessories for infants through preteens. The store features clothing by local designers and offers hand smocking as well as limited editions. Boys' sizes range from infant through size 16, and girls' sizes run from infant through preteen 16. The shop also offers a baby shower registry and can assist with customizing gift baskets for newborns. The playroom, outfitted with television and VCR, is inviting and helps make shopping fun for the whole family.

Genuine Kids

The Outlet Mall on Richmond Road
(757) 565-4625.

Discount clothing for girls sizes 2 to 6X and 7 to 16, and clothing for boys sizes 2 to 7 and 8 to 20.

Scotland House

430 Duke of Gloucester Street in Merchants Square
(757) 229-7800.

Beautiful fine apparel for children imported from Scotland, England, Ireland, and Wales.

Today's Child

The Williamsburg Outlet Mall on Richmond Road (757) 565-2100.

This outlet store carries children's clothing from infant sizes through teens.

Trader Kids

The Williamsburg Outlet Mall on Richmond Road (757) 565-4625.

The store carries the Boston Trader label for infants and children.

Books

Book Cellar

5707 Richmond Road in the Berkeley Commons Shopping Center (757) 565-6212.

Publishers' overstocked titles are carried by this store, so prices are good. There is a nice selection of children's books.

Colonial Williamsburg Book Store

Colonial Williamsburg Visitor Center (757) 229-1000.

A wonderful selection of historical and biographical books for children can be found here. There are books about colonial crafts, music, history, historical figures, and cut-and-assemble colonial coloring books. Souvenir shirts, colonial hats, records and tapes of eighteenth-century music, and souvenir postcards are also for sale.

Marie's Book Store

1915 Pocahontas Trail (757) 564-3541.

Marie's features a separate room for children's books. Books are arranged by age and by grade level. Two comfortable wicker chairs invite leisurely browsing.

Publisher Warehouse

The Outlet Mall on Richmond Road (757) 565-3256.

The store carries children's books at discount prices.

Rizzoli Book Store

Duke of Gloucester Street in Merchants Square (757) 229-9821.

The second floor of this excellent book store carries a complete line of outstanding children's books. While browsing, do make note of the storybook character stuffed animals that are sure to entice and delight.

Toys, Games, Hobbies, and Dolls

Bassett's Christmas Shop

207 Bypass Road (757) 229-7648.

Features a huge selection of unusual Christmas ornaments and trees. There are wonderful Madame Alexander dolls, Dickens' Villages, music boxes, and many gift ideas. Certain to delight children is the model train that runs around the store between the first and second floors. A good place to visit before or after lunch or dinner at the adjoining restaurant.

Christmas Mouse

1430 Richmond Road (757) 229-5002.

Exquisitely decorated Christmas trees, music boxes, dolls, Dickens' Villages, and houses are lovely to see and purchase any time of the year.

Colonial Sports Cards

173 Second Street (757) 253-1309.

The young sports card enthusiast will find football, baseball, basketball, and hockey cards, collector card albums, collector record books, card cases, and card guards. The owners cater their business to children and are eager to answer questions about this popular hobby. The store also carries a large assortment of pogs.

Joe Knows Baseball Cards

Williamsburg Crossing Shopping Center (757) 564-0150.

The store carries all types of sport cards, including baseball, football, basketball, and racing. Non-sport cards, collector supplies, sports collectibles, and pogs are also carried.

Norge Station

7405 Richmond Road, 7 miles west of Colonial Williamsburg (757) 564-7623.

A delightful store for the train enthusiast. Model trains in N scale, HO scale, O gauge, and gauge 1, along with accessories and collectibles, are on display and for sale. There is also a selection of cars and military model kits, NASCAR collectibles, and T-shirts.

School Crossing

29 Williamsburg Crossing on Route 5 (757) 220-8772.

The store carries teacher supplies, educational toys and games, and children's books. Especially nice are the language tapes for children.

Sugar and Spice

2229 Richmond Road (757) 220-1661.

This attractive consignment shop specializes in children's clothing, baby furniture, and maternity clothes. Toys and books are also to be found here.

The Little Patriot

Located opposite the Colonial Williamsburg Visitor Center
(757) 229-1000.

This gift shop specializes in colonial toys, games, and books for children. Both boys and girls delight in wearing the three-cornered hats and colonial mob caps available for purchase. Tin whistles, historic replica pistols and rifles, and colonial games and puzzles are popular items. Fascinating books which describe colonial times and interesting biographies about United States Presidents and other historical figures are for sale. Souvenir T-shirts, unusual pencils and erasers, and other small items are also available.

Toymaker of Williamsburg

Duke of Gloucester Street in Merchants Square (757) 229-5660.

This shop carries a large selection of unusual toys, games, books, puzzles, and models. There is a very nice doll collection as well as doll houses and doll furniture. The store features colonial toys such as dolls dressed in the eighteenth-century manner, guns, hats, fifes, and drums. The stuffed animal collection will delight everyone.

Williamsburg Doll Factory

7441 Richmond Road, 7 miles west of Colonial Williamsburg
(757) 564-9703.

Children of all ages will love the beautiful display of handcrafted dolls in their exquisite gowns. A special treat is to look through the observation window and see the Lady Anne porcelain dolls being created. Doll accessories, doll clothing and wigs, doll houses, and doll furniture are for sale. Of special note is the doll hospital where old or broken dolls can be repaired. Please be aware that this is not a place for a very young child to run freely. Many of the dolls are quite expensive and there are several "Do not touch" signs.

Williamsburg Pottery Factory

Route 60, Lightfoot, 5 miles west of Williamsburg (757) 564-3326.

A trip to Williamsburg would not be complete without a visit to The Pottery. The tour buses lining the parking lot attest to the fact that this is one of the prime shopping meccas on the East Coast. Thirty-two buildings are crammed full of bargains with thousands of items from dishes to plants to craft supplies to furniture to silk flowers to clothing outlets to pecans. Pick up a guide to the buildings at the entrance.

Items of special interest to children can be found in the Solar 2 building. Here are toys and games, collector dolls, miniature doll furniture and doll houses, as well as a hobby shop and model train shop. An inexpensively priced café located in the building offers hot dogs, barbecue, salads, ice cream, soft drinks, and snack items. Restroom facilities are also located within the building.

Restaurants

Eating out with children *can* be a convivial and pleasurable experience. While it does not necessarily mean being limited to fast-food restaurants, it does mean planning ahead. An early dinner almost (but not quite) guarantees a relaxed atmosphere, unruffled children and adults, pleasant servers, and quicker service.

Read this section for suggestions of restaurants that welcome children, are close to attractions and activities, and are family priced. Restaurants are rated as inexpensive ($), dinner entrees under $7.00; moderate ($$), entrees ranging from $8.00 to $15.00; or expensive ($$$), entrees over $16.00. Unless noted otherwise, restaurants are open daily and accept credit cards.

Hampton

Applebee's Neighborhood Grill and Bar

2159 Coliseum Drive (757) 838-8460 ($$).

A varied menu features soups, salads, sandwiches, entrees, and daily specials. Low-fat entrees are available.

Chamberlin Hotel

Fort Monroe (757) 723-6511 ($$).

This lovely old hotel overlooking the water is a good spot for children to practice their table manners. The dining room is elegant without being stuffy and is a charming spot for breakfast, lunch, or dinner. Combine it with a visit to the nearby Casemate Museum or before or after a band concert at adjacent Fort Monroe Park. In addition to menu entrees, there is a large buffet which includes fried chicken, the perennial favorite of most children.

Chuck E. Cheese

4027 W. Mercury Blvd. (757) 827-9150 ($).

A great place for a family to eat pizza and be entertained at the same time. On stage are large, life-like, singing animated characters. Children love to play the video games and ride the motorized rides which are geared more for the young set. Birthday parties are very popular here and come complete with birthday cake and ice cream. A live Chuck E. Cheese walks around greeting the children.

Ming Gate I & II

Two Locations: 2800 W. Mercury Blvd. and 3509 Kecoughtan Road (757) 826-0820 and 723-9572 ($-$$).

Featured are Mandarin, Szechwan, and Hunan cuisine. The restaurants are located close to Bluebird Gap Farm and shopping.

Old Country Buffet

2302 W. Mercury Blvd. (757) 825-0340 ($).

A family restaurant which features an all-you-can-eat buffet. There is one set price for adults and an interesting price structure for children aged 2 to 10. At present, the rate is 35 cents times the child's age for lunch and 40 cents times the child's age for dinner. There is a large selection of hot foods such as meats, chicken, fish, vegetables, soups, and hot breads. The salad bar has a complete line of salad greens, potato salad, cole slaw, macaroni salad, and all the fixings. There are numerous desserts to choose from and a help-yourself beverage bar. Credit cards are not accepted.

Olive Garden

1649 W. Mercury Blvd. (757) 825-8874 ($$).

The restaurant offers a wide variety of pasta dishes. Entrees come with all-you-can-eat salad and warm bread sticks. A children's menu is available. The restaurant is close to Bluebird Gap Farm and shopping.

Red Lobster

1046 W. Mercury Blvd. (757) 838-6062 ($$).

This large, attractive seafood restaurant is close to Bluebird Gap Farm and shopping. Dress is casual and reservations are not required. The separate children's menu is filled with games and puzzles to help keep youngsters entertained as they wait for their popcorn shrimp, hamburger, shrimp on a stick, spaghetti, or other entree.

Top Dog

4024 W. Mercury Blvd. (757) 827-1246 ($).

Located right across Mercury Boulevard from Toys R Us, this very casual restaurant features six kinds of hot dogs, homemade chili, and soft-serve ice cream.

Newport News

Applebee's Neighborhood Grill and Bar

12235 Jefferson Ave. (757) 249-2207 ($$).

See listing under Hampton.

Cheddar's

12280 Jefferson Ave. (757) 249-4000 ($-$$).

Located in Patrick Henry Mall Shopping Center, this restaurant pleases both adults and children. Featured items include salads, soups, sandwiches, and daily specials. A children's menu is offered. Chocolate lovers will enjoy the "Cookie Monster" dessert.

Captain's Gallery

915 Jefferson Ave. (757) 245-1533 ($).

Adjacent to Wharton's Wharf Cruises, this is a very pleasant and informal spot to enjoy a seafood or other type of sandwich. Children enjoy having lunch or dinner on the sun deck when the weather is nice. Credit cards are not accepted.

Cracker Barrel

12357 Hornsby Lane (757) 249-3020 ($-$$).

Located across from Patrick Henry Mall. For additional information see listing under Williamsburg.

Hoss's Steak and Sea House

11985 Jefferson Ave. (757) 249-1058 ($-$$).

Steaks, seafood, and chicken are the featured items. Soups, salads and bread pudding are made in-house. Help yourself to the all-you-care-to-eat salad, soup, and bread bar. The fruit and dessert bar features soft-serve frozen yogurt.

Hot Dog King

10725 Jefferson Ave. and 12838 Jefferson Ave.
(757) 595-1630 and 874-2556 ($).

Regular-sized and foot-long hot dogs, hamburgers, and barbecue just about complete the menu of this very busy small establishment. It is located close to museums, parks, and shopping.

Lotus Pond Szechwan Restaurant

12460 Warwick Blvd. (757) 591-0800 ($-$$).

Featuring Chinese cuisine, the restaurant is located near the Mariners' Museum and the Virginia Living Museum.

Old Country Buffet

14346 Warwick Blvd. (757) 874-2556 ($).

Close to shopping. See listing under Hampton.

Red Lobster

14859 Warwick Blvd. (757) 874-3434 ($$).

The restaurant is located close to the Fort Eustis Transportation Museum and Newport News Park. For additional information, see listing under Hampton.

Rock-Ola Café

12648 Jefferson Ave. (757) 874-4847 ($$).

Located near Newport News Park and shopping. The restaurant offers burgers, salads, sandwiches, and entrees. A section of the menu is devoted to children and features items such as junior cheeseburgers and chicken fingers.

Ruby Tuesday

Patrick Henry Mall (757) 249-1829 ($$).

This family restaurant features a large selection of dinner entrees, as well as soups, salads, sandwiches, and a large salad bar.

Ryan's Family Steak House

11883 Jefferson Ave. (757) 930-4400 ($).

Top off an outing to the Virginia Living Museum, the Mariners' Museum, or Deer Run Park with lunch or dinner at this buffet-style family restaurant. The buffet contains a selection of hot entrees and vegetables, a huge selection of salads, and a wonderful dessert bar. Try the cinnamon buns!

Williamsburg

The city of Williamsburg is unique in its wide range of eating establishments. For example, children usually enjoy pancakes, and Williamsburg is "pancake paradise." Approximately 20 pancake restaurants tempt the appetite with everything from plain to fruit-filled to chocolate-chip pancakes. In addition, busy Richmond Road is saturated from one end to the other with a variety of restaurants. Some local favorites are the focus of this section.

A Good Place to Eat

410 Duke of Gloucester Street (757) 229-4370 ($).

This fast-food restaurant right in Merchants Square offers both indoor and very attractive outdoor seating.

Bassett's Restaurant

207 Bypass Road (757) 229-3614 ($$).

Adjacent to Bassett's Classic Christmas Shop. Hamburgers, salads, seafood, steaks, and daily specials are offered and a children's menu is available.

Beethoven's Inn

467 Merrimac Trail (Route 143) in the Family Dollar Shopping Center (757) 229-7069 ($).

A local favorite, Beethoven's is a New York-style delicatessen that features reubens, sailors, subs, and French onion soup. Classical music and a selection of board games help diners unwind and relax after a busy day of sightseeing. Credit cards are not accepted.

Bob Evans

1735 Richmond Road (757) 229-2470 ($$).

The popular family restaurant is open for breakfast, lunch, and dinner. There is also a large country gift shop that invites browsing. The restaurant is located close to Mini Golf America.

Candle Factory

7521 Richmond Road (757) 564-0803 ($-$$).

Located right in the Candle Factory complex, this casual restaurant is open for breakfast, lunch, and dinner and offers lunch and dinner specials every day. A children's menu is available.

Cheese Shop

Merchants Square (757) 220-0298 or 220-1324 ($).

If asked for a recommendation for a good, inexpensive lunch in the Historic Area, locals are likely to suggest a made-to-your-order sandwich at this convenient shop. When your order is ready, carry it outside and enjoy the large sandwich under one of the patio umbrella tables. Ready for dessert? Try Baskin-Robbins right next door.

Colonial Williamsburg Taverns

Colonial Williamsburg (757) 229-2141 ($$$).

Choose from among four taverns for a not-to-be-missed eighteenth-century dining experience served by costumed waiters. During dinner, diners are regaled with eighteenth-century music and song by costumed entertainers. Call the above number to make the necessary reservations at Christiana Campbell's Tavern, Chownings Tavern, the King's Arms Tavern, or Shield's Tavern.

Cracker Barrel

200 Bypass Road (757) 220-3384 ($-$$).

This large and busy family restaurant is close to the Historic Area. Breakfast, lunch, and dinner are served, and breakfast is available all day. There is a separate children's menu. This is a very popular restaurant and there is usually a wait of about 30 minutes. To help pass the time, have a "sit" in one of the attractive rocking chairs outside, or browse about the very nice country gift store.

Downtown Shortstop Cafe

500 Jamestown Road (757) 220-0279 ($-$$).

A favorite of the locals, this relatively small restaurant is adjacent to the Historic Area and the College of William and Mary. Dress is casual and reservations are not required. Homemade soups, salads, sandwiches, hamburgers, submarines, dinner entrees, as well as delicious desserts are offered. There are always a few "heart-healthy" items on the menu, and a children's menu is available.

Dynasty

1621 Richmond Road (757) 220-8888 ($-$$).

An extremely attractive, award-winning Chinese restaurant. Lazy Susan tables are available for large parties. Children love to spin the various entrees (and occasionally a toy or two) around the table. Reservations for dinner are suggested.

Friendly Family Restaurant

1803 Richmond Road (757) 220-2635 ($)

The bucket of crayons given to each child to use on the puzzle side of the kids' menu helps to make waiting to be served a lot more pleasant for both children and parents. The menu offers such welcome kids' fare as pizza, chicken, macaroni and cheese, hamburgers, and hot dogs. Top off dinner with a cone-head sundae.

La Tolteca

5351 Richmond Road (757) 253-2939 ($).

A very casual restaurant serving authentic Mexican food. It is close to the shopping malls on Richmond Road.

Milano's

1635 Richmond Road (757) 220-2527 ($$).

This attractive restaurant offers Italian cuisine such as pasta, veal, chicken, sandwiches, an all-you-can-eat spaghetti bar, and a salad bar. A children's menu is available. Dress is casual and reservations are not required.

New York Deli

6572 Richmond Road (757) 564-9258 ($).

Stop in this self-service deli for homemade pizza, huge delicatessen sandwiches and subs, strombolis, gyros, and salads. It is located near The Pottery and Go-Karts Plus. Credit cards are not accepted.

Peking

Two locations: 5601-12 Richmond Road in the Ewell Station Shopping Center, and 122 Waller Mill Road in the Kingsgate Green Shopping Center (757) 565-1212 or 229-2288 ($-$$).

This award-winning Chinese restaurant features Peking, Szechuan, and Hunan cuisine, and is a favorite of the locals at both locations. Dress is casual and reservations are suggested for dinner. Food is served buffet style at the Richmond Road location.

Pelican

5699 Richmond Road, Berkeley Commons Shopping Center (757) 565-2054 ($).

Situated right in the Berkeley Commons Shopping Center, this restaurant offers shoppers a respite of soups, sandwiches, and salads. Credit cards are not accepted.

Pierce's Pitt Bar-B-Que

Rochambeau Drive (757) 565-2955 ($).

Serving Williamsburg since 1971, this local favorite offers huge barbecue sandwiches and platters, hot dogs, coleslaw, potato and macaroni salads, and baked beans. Eat inside or take advantage of a lovely day by eating at one of the picnic tables on the porch. Somewhat out of the way but worth the trip, it is not far from Waller Mill Park.

Prince George Espresso & Roastery

433 Prince George Street
(757) 220-6670 ($).

Go right downstairs to the small dining room of this very casual restaurant which serves lunches of soups, salads, and a nice selection of sandwiches on freshly baked breads. Fresh gourmet pastries are offered as well as a huge variety of coffees, teas, hot chocolates, and sodas. The restaurant is very convenient to the Historic Area.

Red Lobster

2000 Richmond Road (757) 221-8127 ($$).

For additional information see listing under Hampton.

Royal Gardens

1203 Richmond Road (757) 229-7778 ($-$$).

Very popular with the locals, the restaurant features a full range of Chinese appetizers, soups, and entrees.

Ruby Tuesday

1840 Richmond Road (757) 229-1829 ($$).

See listing under Newport News.

Seasons Cafe

110 South Henry Street (757) 259-0018 ($$).

Wonderfully located right off Merchants Square, this delightful restaurant offers a varied menu of entrees, soups, salads, and sandwiches. If you prefer, you can make a meal from the extensive salad bar. A good choice for lunch, dinner, or an afternoon pick-me-up while touring Colonial Williamsburg. Both indoor and outdoor seating is offered.

Sakura Japanese Seafood and Steak House
601 Prince George Street (757) 253-1233 ($$).

Enjoy Hibachi-style cooking at communal tables. A grand show of flashing knives, eggs sliced in mid-air, and cooking implements tossed into the chef's hat delights and amuses both children and adults. The dinner is a wide-eyed experience for children as the chefs usually do their best to be especially attentive to any youngsters at the table. The restaurant will also cater children's birthday parties. It is located conveniently close to the Historic Area.

Sal's Italian Restaurant and Pizzeria
Two Locations: 1242 Richmond Road, Williamsburg Shopping Center and 264 McLaws Circle, Festival Marketplace (near Busch Gardens) (757) 220-2641 or 229-0337 ($-$$).

Fanciers of Italian food will enjoy calzone, subs, pasta, seafood, veal, and pizza. There is a children's menu for ages 10 and under.

Sal's Piccolo Forno Italian Restaurant
835 Capitol Landing Road (757) 221-0443 ($-$$).

A very popular family restaurant, Sal's features pizza, subs, and a variety of pastas and veal entrees.

Second Street
140 Second Street (757) 220-2286 ($-$$).

A sandwich board permits patrons to select any two meats, two cheeses, and the type of bread to design their own sandwiches. Also on the menu are hamburgers, Italian food, and seafood. There is a menu for children under 12. The restaurant is casual and reservations are not needed.

Sportman's Grill
240 McLaws Circle (757) 229-6060 ($-$$).

This casual restaurant located near Busch Gardens offers soups, salads, sandwiches, and more substantial entrees. A children's menu is available.

That Seafood Place
1647 Richmond Road (757) 220-3011 ($$).

Specializing in seafood entrees, there is also the "sardine can" salad bar which offers 30 items for both lunch and dinner. There are nightly specials and a children's menu is available. Reservations are not required and the dress is casual.

The Polo Club

135 Colony Square, Colony Square Shopping Center
(757) 220-1122 ($-$$).

Hamburgers, sandwiches, salads, quiche, omelettes, and hot entrees are served in this attractive restaurant. A children's menu is available.

The Whaling Company

494 McLaws Circle, near Busch Gardens
(757) 229-0275 ($$-$$$).

Located close to Busch Gardens, this lovely restaurant specializes in fresh seafood. Daily fresh fish catches are listed along with the regular menu. There is a children's menu available. Reservations are requested for dinner.

Wythe Candy and Gourmet Shop

Shops on Wythe Green on Richmond Road near The Pottery
(757) 565-1151 ($).

Freshly made chicken and tuna salads and sandwiches, as well as hot dogs are available in this shop located across from The Pottery. Have an ice cream cone while browsing about the candy shop. Be sure to check out the observation window and watch the candy-making process.

Further Afield

Below are some restaurant suggestions to help complete plans for day-trip outings. Fast-food and other choices are also available in most areas.

Broadway Cafeteria

120 E. City Point Road, Hopewell (757) 458-1700 ($).

Featuring "down-home" entrees such as chicken, roast beef, meat loaf, and spaghetti, the whole family will enjoy eating here.

Captain's Cove

910 21st Street, Hopewell (757) 452-1368 ($$).

If you're looking for seafood, the Captain's Cove offers a nice variety. Steaks, chicken, and ribs are also on the menu.

Coach House Tavern

Berkeley Plantation on Route 5, Charles City County
(757) 829-6003 ($$).

Lunch at this charming restaurant is a must when visiting the plantations. Specializing in game and fresh seafood, it is an elegant yet friendly restaurant for children to practice their good table manners without being overwhelmed. Reservations are not necessary for lunch. The restaurant turns quite elegant for dinner and is recommended for adults only as entrees can be quite expensive. Reservations are required for dinner.

Doumar's

19th to 20th Streets and Monticello Ave., Norfolk
(757) 627-4163 ($).

Nostalgia lovers and children will enjoy this 1950's style drive-in restaurant, or if preferred, customers can dine inside. Pork barbecue, hamburgers, Taylor pork roll, and hot dogs are the mainstays of this well-known restaurant. Accompany your sandwich with an old-fashioned milk shake, egg nog, or ice cream soda. Whatever you do, save room for an ice cream cone, an original Doumar creation. The hand-rolled cone was first sold at the St. Louis Exposition in 1904—and the cones are still made by hand. Closed Sunday.

Nick's Seafood Pavilion

Water Street, Yorktown
(757) 887-5269 ($$-$$$).

A venerable institution in Yorktown, most visitors have lunch or dinner here while touring the Yorktown sights. Seafood is the specialty, but there are other entrees as well. The Greek salads are enormous. Be sure to examine the statuary decorating the rooms.

Portside

Water Street, Portsmouth (757) 393-5111 ($-$$).

Located on the waterfront are open-air stalls offering a variety of food and ice cream.

The Surry House Restaurant

Highway 31 East, Surry (757) 294-3389 ($-$$).

A "must" stop for lunch while touring Surry, this restaurant gives hungry diners the opportunity to sample Southern cuisine such as peanut soup, ham specialties, seafood, and peanut raisin pie. A special treat for youngsters is the peanut butter sandwich. Costumed servers bring out a large cutting board containing all the "fixins" for a peanut butter sandwich smorgasbord. Pick your favorite combination to make a do-it-yourself sandwich. Slices of white and brown bread, a jar of peanut butter, honey, bacon, raisins, jelly, banana, apple wedges, and cheese are certain to entice any "junior gourmet" or even the "picky" eater. Before leaving, be sure to ask for your bag of bread to feed the sea gulls on the return ferry ride to Jamestown.

Virginia Beach

Choose from the many seafood, delicatessen, and fast-food restaurants both on and off the boardwalk.

Waterside

Waterside Drive, Norfolk (757) 627-3300 ($-$$$).

Just about any type of food and price range desired can be found here. For inexpensive prices and lots of variety visit the food court on the lower level. Here are seafood, salads, delicatessen, Chinese, Mexican, Greek, hamburgers, ice cream, espresso, and more. On the stage are likely to be music, dancing, puppet shows, face painting, and other types of entertainment. Seafood and other types of restaurants are also located in the mall, making it likely that your family will find just the right sort of ambiance to please all members.

Ice Cream

A Good Place to Eat

440 Duke of Gloucester Street, Williamsburg
(757) 229-4370.

Enjoy a delicious ice cream cone or sundae either outdoors under a shady umbrella or indoors during inclement weather.

Baskin-Robbins

416 Prince George Street, Williamsburg
(757) 229-6385.

Always 31 ice cream flavors from which to choose. In addition to regular ice cream, there are also light, sugar-free, and fat-free ice creams as well as low-fat and fat-free frozen yogurt.

Ben & Jerry's

Two locations: 3044 Richmond Road, Williamsburg (next to West Point Pepperell in the Patriot Plaza Shopping Center) and 3097 Pocahontas Trail (Route 60 East) (757) 565-3800 and 255-0180.

A large selection of wonderful flavors of all-natural ice cream, frozen yogurt, and ices.

Carvel Ice Cream and Bakery

Two locations: 1064 W. Mercury Blvd., Hampton and 409 Denbigh Blvd., Newport News (757) 827-1956 and 874-8447.

Soft ice cream, ice cream, and desserts.

Friendly Family Restaurant

1803 Richmond Road, Williamsburg (757) 220-2635.

Ice cream cones, sundaes and toppers, ice cream sodas, frozen yogurt, fribbles, and more.

Index

Barbara M. Wohlford, a Williamsburg teacher and historical interpreter, has always felt strongly about the value of field trips for children. She has long worked with families and school groups, bringing a sense of adventure and discovery to all her activities.

Mary L. Eley of Newport News, who has taught preschool for the physically and mentally disadvantaged, understands the need for children's activities that are stimulating, educational, and fun. Having travelled extensively with her own children, she knows the importance of knowing where such activities can be found.

Notes